To Mary

Elizabeth Johnson

Redefining Retirement
New Realities for Boomer Women

Redefining

Retirement

New Realities for Boomer Women

Dr. Margret Hovanec
Elizabeth Shilton

Second Story Press

Library and Archives Canada Cataloguing in Publication

Hovanec, Margret, 1941-
Shilton, Elizabeth, 1948-
Redefining retirement : new realities for boomer women / by
Margret Hovanec and Elizabeth Shilton.

Includes bibliographical references.
ISBN 978-1-897187-21-0

1. Women—Retirement—Canada. 2. Baby boom generation—Canada.
3. Retirement—Canada—Planning. I. Hovanec, Margret, 1941- II. Title.

HQ1063.2.C3S48 2007   646.7'90820971   C2007-900963-8

Edited by Doris Cowan
Designed by Melissa Kaita
Cover photos © Guillermo Perales Gonzalez/istockphoto.com

Printed and bound in Canada

Second Story Press gratefully acknowledges the support of the Ontario Arts Council
and the Canada Council for the Arts for our publishing program. We acknowledge
the financial support of the Government of Canada through the Book Publishing
Industry Development Program.

Canada Council   Conseil des Arts
for the Arts   du Canada

Published by
Second Story Press
20 Maud Street, Suite 401
Toronto, ON
M5V 2M5
www.secondstorypress.ca

Contents

To my husband, Peter Warrian, and my mother, Anna — M.H.

To David, and to my mother — E.S.

CHAPTER 1

Retirement:
The Next Frontier
for Working Women

THE BOOMERS ARE RETIRING … INCLUDING WOMEN

You can't open a newspaper these days without confronting apocalyptic headlines about the impending wave of retiring baby boomers. Those of us born between 1946 and 1964 are the demographic time bomb: whatever we do has always been the Next Big Thing. And what we're going to do next is retire, *en masse*. The oldest boomers have just turned sixty, and over the next fifteen years we will transform the way the world works, plays, and does business. The health care system, the housing market, and the public and private pension systems will all have to adapt to us. The graying of the boomers has begun.

Many of these retiring boomers will be women. This fact has been largely unobserved, or at least unnoted, by both academic and popular experts on the issue. It's taken for granted that women work, and will retire as a matter of course. So *of course* the wave of boomer retirees will include women.

But we are about to experience something unique in our history — not just the first wave of boomers retiring, but also the first wave ever of *women* retiring in significant numbers. Let's not forget that back in the 1960s, before the boomers began to embark on jobs and careers, the Canadian workforce was almost 80 percent male. By 1976, however, it was 37 percent female, and the percentage of women has been climbing steadily since then. In 2003 almost half (47 percent, according to Statistics Canada) of the Canadian workforce was female. Although working women are now very much the rule rather than the exception, the boomer generation is the first to include a significant proportion of women who have spent most of their lives in the paid workforce. Not all of us did, of course, and some early boomers chose lives not so very different from our mothers': marriage, homemaking, and raising children. But over the years most of those women too joined the world of work, some part time, some determined to build careers in their forties, or even their fifties. The majority of the boomer women who are now making retirement plans are the first critical mass of women ever to retire from the workforce in Canada.

> The entry of large numbers of women into the paid workforce has been one of the dominant social trends in Canada over the last half century.
>
> Statistics Canada, *Women in Canada*, 2000

The women who entered the labor force in the 1960s, '70s, and '80s saw themselves as pioneers, the first generation of women to "have it all" — serious, fulfilling careers, good incomes, satisfied spouses, large, tastefully decorated homes, handsome, clever and well-adjusted children. We wanted something better than the lifestyles of our mothers and grandmothers, those domesticated women who stayed home to raise their children — us — instead of venturing out into the wider world of paid employment. We wanted to blaze a path for women into the "real" world, the world of serious work.

And we had to work hard to achieve our goals. "Having it all," it turned out, wasn't a cakewalk. We read Simone de Beauvoir and Betty Friedan, Germaine Greer and *Ms.* magazine, and we knew that our menfolk were not going to forgo their workplace privileges or take on their share of the housework without a struggle. There were challenges. But as a generation, we took on those challenges, and in our different ways we did surmount them. We found our path, and we changed society. Women are a visible and formidable presence in Canadian workplaces now. Our work is a critical component of the economy.

And now we, the pioneers, are reaching the age at which most Canadian workers are thinking about retirement. We were the first generation of women to enter the workforce in massive numbers, and now we will be the first generation of women to retire in massive numbers. We led the way in breaking down the entry barriers. Now we will have to lead the rush for the exits.

THE OLD RETIREMENT AND THE NEW RETIREMENT

We were short on female role models in the world of work, and we'll be equally short on female role models for retirement. The generations of retirees before us were men, and we've had plenty of unfortunate experience in our working lives with the pitfalls of trying to squeeze ourselves into male molds. But even if we were tempted to follow that road again in retirement, we've got other obstacles facing us, because it's not likely that the old models are going to work for very much longer, even for men. It's just our luck that we, the vanguard, will have to create a female retirement model in a world that is changing dramatically for all older Canadians, male or female.

The concept of retirement has evolved considerably over the years since it first entered cultural consciousness with the industrial revolution in the nineteenth century. Initially, with the exception of the very few businessmen who struck it rich and retired to enjoy their wealth, retirement wasn't something working people planned. It simply happened.

Industrial labor was hard and debilitating, and there came a time in every worker's life when his body simply wore out — that is, if he didn't die first from disease or accident. A worn-out worker ceased to be profitable to his employer, and he could no longer find a job. If he was thrifty and lucky, he might have something put by for his old age. Or perhaps he had adult children who would care for him until he died. If he had none of these resources, he and his spouse had to look to the state for their maintenance — the dreaded poorhouse or its equivalent.

In this world, retirement was feared rather than welcomed. Public pensions, where they existed, were a form of welfare. Canada's first Old Age Pensions Act, introduced in 1927, allocated benefits only to the most needy. Private pensions too were rooted in the charitable concept of the relief of poverty for those who had lost the capacity for self-support. That stock character of Victorian fiction, the pensioned-off family retainer, came from a tradition of *noblesse oblige;* only a lucky few received such pensions and the wealthy families who recognized a moral duty to take care of those members of the lower classes who depended on them directly would have strongly resisted any move to make such pensions payable as a matter of legal entitlement. There was no sense, in this world, that society should pool its resources to take care of its oldest members on a footing of equality.

That was the *Old Retirement*. At the beginning of the twentieth century, few workers sought it. And in an era in which average life expectancy was not much more than fifty years, few experienced it — they didn't live long enough.

As the twentieth century progressed, however, a rather different notion of retirement was born. After World War II there was an economic boom, as well as a baby boom. Incomes for ordinary working people improved greatly. Surplus earnings could be saved and invested. A portion of those savings went into newly burgeoning private pension plans, and employees who were fortunate enough to be members of such plans began to see their pensions, quite properly, as an earned benefit, a right and not an act of charity. Public retirement pension schemes expanded greatly. The possibility of funding some years of pleasurable leisure after a working life was now well within reach for more than just the very wealthy. And predictably, workers responded to this new environment by leaving the workforce earlier and earlier, as soon as they were financially able to do so.

One financial services company advertised early retirement as "Freedom Fifty-Five," although even in its heyday in the 1970s and '80s the average age of retirement never crept much below where it currently rests, just above age sixty-one. These retirees had worked through the economic boom years after the war and their pensions (usually the husband's) were comfortable. Let's call this retirement, that of our parents' generation, the *Post-War Retirement*.

During these years, medical science advanced to the point where it had defeated more and more of the health scourges of the past. At the same time that workers were hoping to retire earlier and earlier, life expectancy had increased dramatically.

Life Expectancy for Canadians Born in:	At Birth Women	At Age 65 Women	At Birth Men	At Age 65 Men
1901	53		50	
1921	60.6	+ 13.6	58.8	+ 13.0
1951	70.9	+ 15.0	66.4	+ 13.3
1971	76.4	+ 17.6	69.4	+ 13.8
1991	80.9	+ 19.9	74.6	+ 15.8
1999	81.7	+ 20.3	76.3	+ 16.5

Sources: *Women's Health Surveillance Report, Mortality: Life And Health Expectancy of Canadian Women,* and *Women and Men in Canada: A Statistical Glance,* 2003 Edition, Statistics Canada and Status of Women Canada

So where does that leave *us*? Retired workers can now expect to live much longer than they did in earlier generations. In 1900, the average length of retirement was just one year, and it was usually accompanied by physical debility and decline. Our parents, on average, lived longer and healthier lives than our grandparents. If present patterns continue, a Canadian who retires today in good health at age fifty-five would be well advised to plan for a retirement lasting twenty-five to thirty years. Thirty years! Retirement is now a stage of life that may last, for many of us, as long or longer than our time in the workforce. That's a lot of life to finance without a steady income. And because of general improvements in health care, nutrition, industrial safety, and the ergonomics of work, most of us can expect to live out much of that time in reasonably good health.

Welcome to the *New Retirement*.

THE CHALLENGES POSED BY THE NEW RETIREMENT

In the world of the New Retirement, we'll live much longer, and we'll be much healthier. How will all of this affect our planning?

Our retirement funds will have to last much longer

Longer retirements won't come cheap. We boomers have indulged ourselves throughout our lives. We have high expectations. We want to continue to consume abundantly. Our needs for health care and social services will increase as we age. All of this will cost money, lots of money.

Who's going to pay for our retirement? Good question! Part of the tab for the New Retirement will be publicly funded: Canadian taxpayers will be footing that bill. This wouldn't be cause for concern if we could count on the ratio of workers to retirees — the "dependency ratio" — staying constant. But that ratio won't stay constant, of course. The baby boom is the "pig in the python." The younger boomers, who are still in their forties and early fifties, are now at their peak earning power and will continue to contribute substantial tax dollars for another decade or more, but the next generations — our children and grandchildren — are much smaller. The dependency ratio now stands at 4.6 workers for every retiree. When the boomers leave the workforce, that ratio will drop sharply. By 2050, predictions are that the ratio might fall as low as 1.78 workers for every retiree. If those in the workforce are expected to pay for the pension and health care costs of those who are not, the tax burden on earners will be heavy indeed. Will the next generations be willing to bear that burden?

We are fortunate in Canada. Our Canada Pension Plan is solid and solvent. Those of us now planning retirement can probably count on our public pension to fulfill its promise for as long as we need it. But public sources currently fund less than 30 percent of the relatively modest retirement incomes of Canadians. In view of the demographic realities, that percentage is not likely to increase anytime soon. As retirees, it's only realistic to recognize that we will be relying on our own resources to fund most of our retirement income.

Maybe you haven't worried about your retirement income; you feel secure because you're a member of a private pension plan. But unless you live in a bubble, you'll know that private pension plans are struggling these days to remain solvent and deliver the benefits they promised. Even the mighty Ontario Teachers Pension Fund, the largest private pension plan in Canada, had a $6 billion shortfall in 2005. And there may be tougher times ahead for the Teachers Pension Plan. By 2020, there may be only 1.1 working teachers paying into the fund for every retired teacher collecting a pension, down from a 10 to 1 ratio in 1970.

For most of us, it's unlikely, very unlikely, that retirement will mean complete freedom from paid employment, at least not right away. We will be working on at least a part-time basis to supplement our pension incomes. There are other choices — trimming lifestyles, for example. But a life of unbroken leisure throughout a thirty-year retirement is probably not in the cards for most of us.

We'll still have lots more time on our hands

If we leave the workforce at fifty-five, sixty, or even sixty-five, *what are we going to do for the next twenty or thirty years?* That's at least as important as what we're going to live on while we're doing it. The stereotypical Old Retiree sat by the fireplace and nodded away his last year of life. The stereotypical Post-War Retiree played golf or bridge on a cruise ship. What will the New Retiree do?

The options and choices are legion, of course. But we're not just talking about pleasant ways to kill time. We're talking about a significant chunk of our time on this earth. We will need to deploy that time in ways that will provide meaning and satisfaction in our lives. We will need to be challenged. We will need variety. And some of us will also need, throughout at least part of our retirement, to earn income to support ourselves.

We'll need to work hard to stay healthy for as long as we can

We look forward to a long retirement. But a long retirement can be a mixed blessing if it comes with debility and disease. We need to focus not just on the length, but also on the quality of that retirement. Without the stress of full-time work, we can be healthier in retirement than we were before, but we'll have to work at achieving and maintaining good health. And we will also have to plan for the eventuality of failing health, disease, and death.

We'll need durable social support networks

Humans are social animals. We live, grow, and develop within families and communities. Throughout our lives, we have depended on social support networks for our happiness and our sustenance. Those needs won't change when we retire.

Work, for many of us, is an important locus of our social world. When we leave our jobs, we will leave behind a comfortable web of social relationships that have sustained and nourished us. If we're lucky, we'll have family to fall back on. But we can't count on family alone. We need to build social support in our communities. We need friends of all ages. We need to ensure that we do not isolate ourselves from our social supports, and that we do not outlive the networks that sustain us.

Above all, we'll need to be flexible

Sociologists used to think in terms of a three-stage life cycle — school, work, and retirement. By the 1980s, as life expectancy increased, it was clear that "retirement" could no longer be viewed realistically as a single stage of life. Leading gerontologist Bernice Neugarten divided retirees into two categories: the *young old*, the still vigorous and socially integrated retirees between fifty-five and seventy-five, and the *old old*, retirees over seventy-five, no longer able to be active as before and growing socially isolated. Her two categories were widely adopted, but many gerontologists now recognize two additional categories of retirees, the "early retired" (created by splitting those fifty-five to sixty-five from Neugarten's "young old"), and the "older old," those past eighty-five. Realistically, most of us will experience retirement in several of these phases. Our resources, wants, and needs will change dramatically over that time. Our circumstances will change. Our ability to work will change. Our health will change. The world will change, probably dramatically. And we will change, experiencing personal development and growth in the years of leisure and freedom that we have earned, at least we hope so. Our planning will need to take all that into account. Our retirement will include periods when we are energetic and mobile and still very employable. It will include periods when our health fails or we no longer have any interest in paid work. It will include catastrophic life events, like the death of a partner. Flexibility will be the order of the day.

WOMEN HAVE DIFFERENT RETIREMENT PLANNING ISSUES

Dora Costa, in her leading study, *The Evolution of Retirement*, says:

> "my focus… is on the retirement of men… As late as the 1970s,… retirement was simply not a meaningful concept for women… The experience of future cohorts [of women] — cohorts that have spent their entire careers in the labour force — is likely to be different. For them, retirement will be a meaningful concept."

The challenges posed by the New Retirement will confront both women and men. There's no doubt that women and men facing retirement have much in common. But women also face retirement planning issues that men do not face. There have been real and substantial differences between our life experiences and those of our male counterparts, both inside and outside the workforce. And those differences matter for retirement planning. The fact that we are women has affected profoundly how we have lived our lives. It will have an equally profound effect on the issues and factors we must take into account in planning for our retirement.

Facts About Canadian Women
- Women constitute **50.4%** of the total population:
- Women constitute **55.5%** of the population age 65-84
- Women constitute **69.5%** of the population age 85 and over
- Average annual income for women: **$24,400**
- Average annual income for men: **$39,300**
- **8.7%** of women 65+ are poor
- **4.4%** of men 65+ are poor
- **18.9%** of unattached women 65+ are poor
- **14.7%** of unattached men 65+ are poor
- **45.5%** of women spend more than 15 hours a week on housework
- **23.3%** of men spend more than 15 hours a week on housework

Statistics Canada, *Women in Canada: A Gender-Based Statistical Report*, 5th edition, 2006. "Poor" means an income after tax below StatsCan's Low Income Cut-off.

Women will have less money to retire on

Women will be retiring from a work world in which women's battle for equality, and in particular equal pay, is far from won. Working women now considering retirement earned between 59 and 72 cents for every dollar earned by men throughout their working lives. This has obviously affected their ability to save for their retirement.

About one-third of working Canadians retire with a private pension, and women, after lagging behind for many years, are now almost as likely as men to be in this group, largely because they are so heavily represented in public sector employment. But women as a group have spent fewer years in the workforce, and have earned less. Because pension benefit formulas are normally based on earnings and length of service, women will have lower pensions.

And they won't be able to close the pension income gap with RRSP income. Because women have lower earnings, they have less RRSP contribution room. They also have less money to fill that contribution room. It's not surprising, then, that fewer women than men contribute to RRSPs, and those who do contribute make smaller contributions. Furthermore, boomer women who contributed to RRSPs during their early working years may have collapsed or drawn down on those plans to fund periods of maternity and parenting leave. All of these factors mean they will have much less put aside for retirement.

Women will have access to fewer financial resources than men from which to fund their retirements. Compared to men's, Canadian women's retirement income is currently about 65 cents on the dollar. Unsurprisingly, those figures are very close to that 59 to 72 cents on the male dollar we earned while we were working. While careful financial planning is critical for all retirees, issues of money — where to get it and how to spend it wisely — will be more critical for women retirees than for men.

Women will be retired longer

Women tend to retire earlier than men, often to synchronize retirement with a spouse or to care for an aging parent. And since women live longer than men, their longer life expectancy has important implications for retirement financial planning. A simple but stark illustration: Annuities, which are priced based on life expectancy, yield a lower annual income for women than for men, in return for the same capital investment. Retirement planning for women means figuring out ways to make less money last longer.

Women may have trouble retiring from their "second shift"

Women will also be retiring in a world in which, despite the battles of past decades, they still do the lion's share of the domestic and emotional work in families, regardless of whether or not they also work for pay. If patterns run true to form, in many cases we will have to navigate the social, economic, and psychological shoals of our own departure from the workforce, and at the same time deal with the care, feeding, and emotional nurturance of male partners who are also retiring or retired. If we're not careful, we will also end up with our usual unfair share of the housework, elder care (our parents — usually our mothers — are often still living and need us more now than they ever did before), and the needs of sometimes still-dependent children and grandchildren. We will need to tread carefully and negotiate skillfully to make our retirement time our own.

Women will spend more of their retirement alone

Since women tend on average to be younger than their male partners by about two years, and they have longer life expectancy, women who are married or in long-term relationships with male partners (and that's still the majority of women) can expect their partners to die before them. Realistic retirement planning must address the fact that women are more likely than men to have to spend part of their retirement alone.

Women may have less control over the timing of their retirement

Far more often than men, women report that they made their retirement decision for family rather than work reasons. These women may be leaving the workplace before they're really ready. For women who started careers late, this can mean abandoning a career just when they are coming into their prime, losing out on the satisfaction that comes from a sense of mastery, and forgoing the opportunity to enjoy the privileges they have earned by experience. Late bloomers, leaving careers they feel they've barely started, may find it harder to adapt to the pace of retirement. It may be hard not to resent the family pressures that compelled them to leave the workplace.

Women who are divorced or separated are much more likely to be poor in their old age

Older women who live outside families are much more likely to be among Canada's poor households than those in families: almost 19 percent of unattached women sixty-five and over are poor, compared to 2 percent of older women in families. A recent study conducted out of McMaster University suggests that older women who have been separated or divorced are even more disadvantaged than women who were always single. They are twice as likely to be poor than divorced or separated men in the same age group. These statistics may not be particularly surprising, but they are very sobering nonetheless. Historically, marriage breakdown has been economically devastating for women, while men's financial circumstances often improve after separation or divorce. Demography tells us that the impact of rising divorce rates is only beginning to affect the sixty-five-and-over group; the proportion of older women whose retirement incomes will be depressed by separation or divorce will likely grow in the coming years.

These are real and important issues for women. They're ignored by much of the retirement planning literature. But as women contemplating retirement, we can't afford to just sweep them under the rug.

So let's keep them at the forefront of our planning process, as we work our way through the issues and problems addressed in this book.

REDEFINING RETIREMENT

What will "retirement" mean in this New Retirement?

That's a good question. And you're not the only one struggling with it. Even Statistics Canada finds the notion of retirement elusive these days:

> The concept of retirement is ambiguous. Generally it might be said that it pertains to older persons who have left the labour force with the notion of not returning but rather with the intention of living on the proceeds of investments or pension plans. On the other hand, some would argue that retirement is a state of mind having nothing to do with either separation from the labour force or with source of income.
>
> Source: StatsCan website, 2/7/2007

Statistics Canada, of course, doesn't have the luxury of philosophizing — it's charged with the task of providing Canadians with very concrete information about very concrete issues. Forced to develop a definition that will produce quantifiable data, it has come up with this:

Retired refers to a person who is aged fifty-five and over, is not in the labour force and receives 50% or more of his or her total income from retirement-like sources.

Do you see yourself in this picture? Maybe that definition will work for you. But maybe it won't. It's pretty clear that in the world of the New Retirement, that clean and clear divide — that thick black line — between the world of work and the world of retirement will no longer exist. In the old days, once you announced your retirement and collected your gold watch, you were done with the world of work. All you saw on the horizon was a vast expanse of leisure. In theory, you could do whatever you wanted. That vision of retirement is no longer realistic. Canadians have already begun to choose to work at retirement occupations and lifestyles that would have been unheard of a generation ago. Their choices to pursue paid work have put significant pressure on the definition of retirement.

THE END OF MANDATORY RETIREMENT

Until recently, mandatory retirement at age sixty-five was legal in Canada. Court challenges against this regime of age-based discrimination, launched in the 1980s and '90s under the *Canadian Charter of Rights and Freedoms* were largely unsuccessful: courts were persuaded that mandatory retirement, while discriminatory, was "a reasonable limit demonstrably justifiable in a free and democratic society." Mandatory retirement was, the courts found, part of a complex social contract, largely unwritten, in which workers got cut some slack cut in the last few years of their employment and departed with a pension, as a *quid pro quo* for their "agreement" to retire at sixty-five.

But mandatory retirement doesn't mesh well with the realities of the New Retirement. And those old discriminatory laws are now changing fast. With Ontario's recent move to outlaw mandatory retirement (although age discrimination will still be permitted in some benefit plans), a majority of Canadian provinces now ban the practice. The remaining jurisdictions are not expected to hold out much longer.

Almost 30 percent of Canadians now retired have returned, or will return at some point, to the labor force. For them, retirement may have been virtually indistinguishable — at least on the surface — from any transition from an old job to a new one. And as the period of retirement gets longer and longer, more and more retirees will return to paid work for a whole variety of reasons, including financial necessity. Is a retiree who returns to the workforce still a retiree? Maybe — or maybe not. In addition, consider that a whopping 20 percent of Canadians aged forty-five to fifty-nine, responding to the General Social Survey in 2002, told Statistics Canada that they do not intend to retire at all. Will retirement disappear altogether before we even get there?

Not likely! Twenty percent of Canadians may not intend to retire, but the other 80 percent still do. We didn't come this far simply to return to the Old Retirement, where we work until we drop. But it's clear that the word *retirement* is undergoing a drastic redefinition. It already means different things to different people. It will do so more and more, and even for each individual, its meaning will change over time.

> "When I use a word," Humpty-Dumpty said in a rather scornful tone, "it means just what I choose it to mean — neither more nor less."
>
> *Through the Looking-Glass,* Lewis Carroll

Our retirements will be very much when and what we make them. We will each have to arrive at our own vision of retirement. We'll have to decide for ourselves what we want and need from retirement. Will we go at fifty-five, or even before that? Will we work for pay or won't we? Will we start drawing down on what we have set aside for retirement or will we — can we — leave our retirement nest egg intact for a while longer? Each of us will have to discover how and where those things we want and need are to be found. We won't be buying a standard retirement off the shelf — it will have to be custom designed by each of us.

It's an exciting prospect. But understandably, it's also somewhat daunting. We know our new lives will be full of challenges and we're not sure how prepared we really are to meet those challenges.

In the chapters that follow, we're going to peel back the old definitions and understanding of retirement and examine what retirement will really mean for baby boomer women. In doing so, we'll help you work out what retirement will mean for you.

CHAPTER 2

Planning for
The New Retirement

IDENTITY CRISIS

In addition to practical challenges, retirement will confront us with what can only be called an identity crisis. In modern society, our work tends to define us. What's the first thing a stranger at a party asks when you meet? Almost always, it's "What do you do?" And we all know what that means. Not "What do you do for intellectual or spiritual nourishment?" Not "What gives meaning to your life?" It means "What do you do for money?" When a woman hears the politically correct question "Do you work outside the home?" she also hears the subtext: "Do you do any *real* work?" *Real* work, of course, being work for pay.

It's not just others who define us by what we "do." We often define and value *ourselves* by the same measuring stick. Our jobs have become critical components of our personal identities, and the value of our paid work has become the measure of our value to society. Who will we be when we step out from behind our workplace personae for the last time, when we no longer wear the label "lawyer" or "psychologist" or "nurse" or "teacher"? Will we still be valued members of society? Or will we be nobodies? It's frightening to contemplate.

Men, of course, are not immune to these fears about retirement. But for women, who fought so hard to gain entrée into the "real world" of work, there is a special angst. We share many of the same worries as our male counterparts: worries about money and power, identity and mortality. But in addition, we fear that when we lose the aura that comes with our jobs, our professional status, we will fade back into being "mere women" again. For us, a job and a paycheck bought more than just material goods and peace of mind. They bought independence and respect. As women who surfed into our occupations and professions on the crest of the feminist wave, we fought for our places in the workforce because we saw that the only thing that really counted when the respect and the power were being handed out was whether or not we got paid for what we did with our time. If we didn't contribute to the Gross National Product, we didn't belong to the club. That's why, at the beginning of our working lives, we chose to opt in to the world of work.

Not that we all got what we bargained for. Once inside, we quickly learned that the power and the respect — not to mention the money — are shared unequally in the world of work. Despite our best efforts, women are still faced with unequal pay and the glass ceiling. Look at the corporate appointments announced daily in the *Globe and Mail*'s "Report on Business." The smiling faces of the corporate elite in this country are still, almost always, the faces of men. The door to the inner sanctum is still largely closed. But we have breached the outer walls of the corporate fortress. We have had a significant measure of success.

It's not easy to step away from all of that. It's not easy to let go, voluntarily, of the brass ring we reached for and grasped with such pride all those years ago. We hear the siren song of retirement, and we are not immune to its attractions. But will those attractions — freedom, leisure, a chance to make new choices, to make a new life for ourselves — be adequate compensation for the loss of the job and the paycheck that was our ticket to equality? Will they give us an identity in the world?

MANAGING OUR ANXIETIES

We're feeling anxious. And we've got plenty to be anxious about. But we can't let anxiety control us. Emotion can cloud our judgment and cause us to make bad decisions. We can't afford to have that happen right now.

How can we deal with these anxieties? Cognitive behavioral psychologists tell us that when we are anxious, we tend to overestimate the risks we face, and underestimate the resources we have available to deal with them. (They call this the risk/resource ratio.) For example, when we think about money, anxiety makes us focus on the uncertainties of the stock market, or the possibility that our employer's pension plan is underfunded and our employer will go bankrupt. (In an anxious mode, we tend to concentrate on and exaggerate the negative aspects of our fear.) We think that our only bulwark against a penurious old age will be our government benefits and we return to worrying about that bulwark collapsing. (In an anxious mode, we tend to downplay and ignore positive possibilities. We underrate what else we can do in our circumstances and rather than looking to positive alternatives, we return to "catastrophizing" our risk.) If we were asked in this state of mind to estimate our retirement prospects on a scale of 1 to 10, we might rate our financial risks in retirement as 10 (catastrophic, impossible) and our resources to deal with them at 2 (I'm screwed). Our risk/resource ratio would be 10/2 or 5.

If we took this problem to a cognitive behavioral therapist, she wouldn't tell us not to worry. She'd explain what was going on and work collaboratively with us to reduce the anxiety. She'd explain that our anxieties aren't, and won't be regarded as, groundless. There are real problems here and we need to deal with them. We would work together at exploring the validity of our fears in the risk category. We would also explore alternate ways of looking at our true available resources and abilities. Even if our worst fears were accurate, the focus could be shifted to re-evaluating and exploring and increasing our views of our resources.

Through this process we would shift our risk/resource ratio to something more realistic and manageable. That would most likely result in our feeling less anxious and more able to engage in planning our retirement.

Here's how an exploration of anxiety might go:

- Identify our issues: What are the risks we're worried about? What are our worst fears?

- Gather as much information as possible about the true nature and quality of those risks

- Identify and explore potential solutions for resolving our fears

- Gather as much information as possible about the resources available to implement the solutions we've found

- Develop a strategy, made up of concrete, specific steps toward measurable and achievable goals, to augment our resources and increase our sense of mastery and control over the risks that threaten us

- Test the strategy: Does it work? Does it make us feel more in control of our destiny?

- Make any adaptations and adjustments necessary to ensure that the strategy will really work to manage our risks and assuage our fears

- Check in to see if our sense of anxiety has decreased

You have just been guided through a process to help you reduce your anxiety and formulate alternate ways of looking at your situation.

You'll recognize this process. It's laying the groundwork for planning. The best way to deal with fears and anxieties is to work through them and develop a plan to manage them.

Unfortunately, our instinct is to do just the opposite. One of the most common human defences against fear and anxiety is avoidance — we fear, therefore we avoid. Lots of Canadians, even those who are quite close to retirement, don't have a plan. They are afraid to begin the planning process. They engage in magical thinking: "If I ignore my problems, maybe they'll just go away on their own!" In the face of massive company layoffs, they cash in some RRSP money and book a cruise. But avoidance is what psychologists call a maladaptive strategy. In other words, it usually doesn't work.

So let's start planning. And remember, although we're all neophytes when it comes to retirement, we're not neophytes when it comes to navigating life passages. We've steered our way through childhood, puberty, and adolescence. We've maneuvered through the world of work. We've negotiated many a human relationship: with friends and lovers and spouses and children. We've lived through and dealt with serious illnesses and the death of loved ones. We've built solid resumés, and we're well-qualified for this new challenge.

IDENTIFYING OUR ISSUES

When we worry about retirement, what do we worry about?

First and foremost, we worry about *money*. For most of us, our work has been our means of subsistence. We work to make a living, to put bread on the table, to pay the mortgage, to buy shoes for our children. When we leave our jobs, our most secure source of income will be gone. When we contemplate retirement, we worry about how we will pay the bills. We worry about whether public policy and economic conditions will sweep away our social benefits. We worry about inflation. We worry about whether we will outlive our savings.

But money's not the only thing we worry about. We also worry about what we're going to *do* after we retire. In other words, we worry about — *work*. Our work lies close to the core of our personal identity. We look to our work for validation of our value and competence in the world. We look to work for structure in our days and in our lives. Work meets our unquenchable human need to be useful and productive. Certainly we look forward to leisure, to rest and relaxation in retirement. But we worry about boredom. We worry about our place in the world. Without meaningful work, where will we be?

And then there is our *health*. What's the point of retirement, after all, if we're not healthy enough to enjoy it? Most of us have abused our bodies in the world of work: Bad health habits come with the territory. Stress, late nights, long hours, fast food, the wear and tear of deadlines, or just routines — they've all taken a toll. Retirement will give us the time to work at good health and fitness. But even though we'll have the time, we're not sure that we've got the will power. And we wonder if we've left it too late. We know we can't go on forever — mortality catches up with all of us eventually. We worry about failing health, disease, and death.

And finally, we worry about our *relationships*. We are social beings. We live in families and communities, and we need one another. Our workplace was, for most of us, a comfortable, ready-made community. Over the years, we have probably spent more waking time with our workmates than we have with our families. We worry about how we will negotiate the unfamiliar social world outside the walls of the workplace. We worry about renegotiating relationships with our family. We worry about elderly parents and fledgling children. We worry about widow-hood. We worry about finding ourselves alone.

THE FOUR INGREDIENTS OF SUCCESSFUL RETIREMENT PLANNING

A successful retirement plan will identify and address our anxieties on all these issues. It will also explore positive alternate resources. That means our retirement planning will have four main ingredients.

- A *money plan*, which will focus realistically on finding a balance between retirement expenses and retirement income.
- A *work plan*, which will help us make the best use of that precious resource, time, and find meaning and value in what we do.
- A *health plan,* which will help us to inform and arm ourselves against the lurking threats to our wellness as we age.
- A *relationships plan,* which will help keep us nourished and sustained in our retirement by a durable network of social supports.

In the pages that follow, we'll examine these four ingredients one at a time. First, we'll offer strategies for assessing your finances and ensuring you can make ends meet. Then, we'll approach the important issue of work and how to make it part of a successful retirement. Next, we'll address current issues in seniors' health, and offer practical suggestions for maintaining a healthy lifestyle. And finally, we'll take a look at the relationships, both intimate and social, that will continue to be essential to your health and happiness in retirement.

Armed with this information, you should be able to map out your own successful four-part retirement plan. And you'll have the tools you'll need to modify the plan as you live it. Like a good stew, a good retirement is a unique creation, a matter of blend and balance, bearing the individual stamp of the cook's creativity. Nobody will be able to tell you how to combine and simmer those ingredients to your own taste; you'll have to figure that out for yourselves.

Ready?

CHAPTER 3

Searching for the Balance: Economics 101

> "Annual income twenty pounds, annual expenditure nineteen nineteen six, result happiness. Annual income twenty pounds, annual expenditure twenty pounds ought and six, result misery."
>
> Wilkins Micawber, in Charles Dickens's *David Copperfield*

FEAR OF BECOMING A BAG LADY

No matter how much we've saved, no matter how careful we've been with our money, we all have our moments of panic. Are we doomed to spend our old age alone and destitute, recycling the teabags in a furnished room, trudging every day to the food bank? We know that as women, our chances of ending up old and poor in Canada are statistically significant.

The poverty rate among elderly women has decreased dramatically in Canada over the last twenty-five years. In 1980, more than 25 percent of Canadian women sixty-five and older had low incomes. By 2003, that number was only 8.7 percent. But that's still almost double the figure for men: only 4.4 percent of men sixty-five and over are poor. And women who live alone are far more likely to be poor than women with partners according to *Women in Canada: A Gender-Based Statistical Report*, 5th Edition from Statistics Canada, 2006. It's true that most of the women who currently swell the ranks of the elderly poor belong to the generation previous to ours, and most of them were never in the workforce. But that's small comfort; they are still women, and we see ourselves potentially reflected in the mirror of their diminished lives.

There's a lot of scary stuff out there in the media to feed our anxieties, much of it advertising created by the fearmongering of the financial services industry. We internalize the messages that come at us from all directions in RRSP season and beyond. *If you don't start your retirement savings plan when you're twenty, you're in big trouble! You'll need to have at least $1 million dollars stashed away by the time you retire if you want your retirement income to live as long as you do! Or maybe it's $2 million? $4 million? Even $12.5 million!* Seriously! We didn't make that $12.5 million figure up. The *New York Times,* in a November 4, 2004 article headlined "How to Avoid Living Like a Poor Student at Age 70," calculated that you'd need that much in savings to sustain your lifestyle if your pre-retirement annual income was $500,000. There may be one or two of you out there, so now you know.

If you've got a million put away, congratulations. Or maybe you've got a blue chip pension plan. Maybe you did what the subway posters counsel, and started a registered retirement savings plan when you were twenty. And maybe you earned enough throughout your career to make your maximum RRSP contributions every year, and never withdrew money from your savings to fund a lay-off or a maternity leave, or just because you needed the money. And maybe you didn't borrow money from your RRSP to buy your first house, or to pursue higher education, even though government programs such as the Home Buyers Plan and the Lifelong Learning Plan encouraged you to do those very things. And maybe, just maybe, you didn't buy high and sell low, confuse past performance with future performance, chase last year's winners, or make any of the myriad other elementary investment errors the rest of us did. Maybe your money actually grew at the rate the ads project. You can feel pretty pleased with yourself. But there aren't very many like you out there.

The rest of us are worried that we won't have enough for retirement. So let's address those worries head on.

HOW MUCH IS ENOUGH?

What *is* an adequate retirement income? Do you really have to have a multi-million-dollar retirement fund before you can stop working for a living? How much is enough?

In the next few chapters, we'll take a realistic look at how much money you'll actually need to retire. In Chapter 4 we'll discuss the sources of retirement income most women can expect. Using that information, you'll be able to estimate the income your current resources will produce for you in retirement. Then, in Chapter, 5 we'll look at the other side of the ledger — how much will it cost you to maintain your current lifestyle after retirement. We'll show you how some of your current expenses will diminish or disappear, simply because you aren't in the workforce any more. When we're finished, you'll have a rough but useful fix on how much money you will need in retirement to pay the bills if you continue to live the life you are currently living. With this income and expenditure information, you'll be able to construct what we call a Lifestyle Maintenance Budget, your income/expenditure balance.

If you have a match — if your income covers your expenditures, you're one of the lucky ones. But for others — probably the majority — the numbers won't jive. Your projected retirement income simply won't pay all the bills, if the bills remain at their current level. Are you looking at a cold and comfortless old age unless you stay shackled to your current job until you drop? You may think you have no choice: you simply

Back in 1992 an American couple, Joe Dominguez and Vicki Robin, wrote a book called *Your Money or Your Life: Transforming Your Relationship with Money and Achieving Financial Independence*. This book is not about retirement *per se*. It's about independent living. The authors argue that most of us have allowed our need for money to control us and take away our freedom to do the things that have meaning for us. It's not our *lack* of money that stands between us and our goals, it's our *need* for money. If we needed less, money problems wouldn't stand in the way of our ability to get a life that aligns with our values and aspirations.

Dominguez and Robin set out a nine-step program to help us get control of our relationship with money by developing sustainable lifestyles. Remind you of a certain other twelve-step program we've all heard about? It's probably not a coincidence. The authors believe that North Americans are addicted to money. Like other addictions, the best, and sometimes the only, effective treatment is self-help. We won't lay out their nine steps here (information about how to find this and other sources mentioned can be found in the Further Reading lists at the end of this book). The movement they are associated with has been dubbed the "Voluntary Simplicity" movement — that should give you some clues...

Their program focuses on the concept of "life energy." In simple terms, life energy is time. To acquire goods and services, we sell our life energy in exchange for money. The authors ask each reader to quantify honestly and accurately, taking into account *all* the costs, the amount of life energy that must be expended by him or her to acquire a particular good or service: e.g., how much more it will take to afford the Audi instead of the Corolla, the Rolex instead of the Timex? Then they ask the simple question: is it worth it? If the answer is yes, so be it. The work we have to do to earn the money to pay for what we really want *is* worth it. But if the answer is no, then we need to cut those goods and services out of our lives, in order to conserve our life energy for the pursuits and goals that really do matter to us.

have to stay in the workforce for longer. On your bad days, longer may seem like forever. Should you despair?

No, of course not. You've still got plenty of choices. All that's happened is you've eliminated one option — you know you can't exit the workforce entirely and expect to live in the style to which you've become accustomed, at least not anytime soon. But is that really so bad? Do most retirees really want life after retirement to replicate exactly their life before retirement? Probably not. Most of us think there's lots of room for improvement in our pre-retirement lifestyles. We want a change — that's the point of retirement, after all. And with new lifestyles come new opportunities. Now — at last! — we can rethink the trade-offs we made during our working lives, between time and money, between income and expenditure. Now we can make room in our lives for the things that are really important to us.

If your Lifestyle Maintenance Budget doesn't balance, life can still be good in retirement. You can fix the problem. But to do so, you will need to focus — *really* focus — on the time-money trade-offs required to secure the retirement you really want, right now and for the rest of your life. You'll need to go back to the expense side of your Lifestyle Maintenance Budget and ask yourself some questions. First of all, do I really *need* all these things that I have budgeted for? Do I even *want* them? Above all, do I want them badly enough to make the time/money trade-off and work longer to get them?

In making trade-offs, there is, of course, no "one size fits all." It's about *your* values and *your* personal choices. Only you can decide which trade-offs are worth it *to you*, and which aren't. But to help you get started on what has to be a very customized process, we take you through some time-tested strategies for finding ways to live on less. In Chapter 6, we consider an array of money-saving ideas, both large and small, that will enable you to reduce your cost of living in retirement. If you are still some years away from leaving your job, you might consider implementing some of these ideas now, before you retire, in order to help your retirement savings grow. Some of them are simple, one-time quick fixes that will have very little impact on your lifestyle. Others will be harder work, involving an on-going investment of time, or a willingness to "make do" with less.

In Chapter 7, we focus on one big ticket item — housing. It's a useful illustration of the complexity of retirement planning. The housing decision is certainly about money: your retirement housing choices will have a major impact on your budget. But housing is about much more than money. A good retirement housing decision requires careful consideration of the other three ingredients of retirement planning as well: work, health, and relationships. Our housing choice should give us meaningful opportunities to fulfill our need to work, either for pay or for love. Where we live should enhance, rather than diminish, our ability to maintain and develop meaningful relationships with friends and family. Where we live should be good for our health, allowing us to eat well, be physically active, take good care of ourselves, and have access to good medical care when we need it. In Chapter 7 we discuss a wide range of options, including staying right where you are.

What's right for you, in the matter of where you live and the lifestyle you choose, will depend on your own wants and needs — and your budget. You need to look hard at these choices *now*. You need to be realistic about the trade-offs you're willing to make. If you know you won't be happy without certain special luxuries, you'll need to look harder at the income side of your ledger. If you can't bear to contemplate a spartan future of frugality and penny-pinching, then maybe "voluntary simplicity" just isn't for you. On the other hand, if the idea of cutting expenses in order to free up your time sounds like liberation, you're clearly a candidate for trading off money for time.

Cost-cutting is not the only option for dealing with a gap between income and expenses; maybe you can do a little income-boosting instead. Later in these pages, we look at the other side of the ledger, examining choices available for increasing retirement income. With the help of some of these ideas, you'll find your own equilibrium — the balancing point where you can realize your personal retirement aspirations and pay the bills at the same time. It's not rocket science. It's Economics 101. If there's a gap between your projected income and your projected expenses, you've got to increase your income, reduce your expenses, or both, until you make ends meet.

So let's ditch the fear of becoming a bag lady. It's not helpful. You have choices. Let's get down to the business of considering them.

CHAPTER 4

Where Will Your Money Come From?

THE THREE STREAMS OF CANADIAN RETIREMENT INCOME

In Canada, women can look to three separate sources for their retirement income: (1) the government, (2) private pension plans, and (3) private savings and investments, including Registered Retirement Savings Plans (RRSPs). The contribution each of these streams will make to your personal retirement ledger will depend very much on your own individual circumstances.

Let's say you're a teacher, a hospital nurse, or a public employee. You've been employed for most of your working life in a job that comes with a blue-chip private pension plan; your pension plan contributions will have eaten up most of your annual RRSP contribution room, so private savings like RRSPs will contribute less to your overall retirement income. You'll be entitled to benefits from the Canada Pension Plan, but this won't put as much into your retirement coffers as you might think. You will also be eligible for Old Age Security, although some or all of this OAS benefit may be "clawed back" through the income tax system depending on your overall income level. Chances are that the biggest single contributor to your retirement income will be your private pension.

If you were self-employed for most of your working life — a partner in a large law firm, for example, or an independent businesswoman who ran a neighborhood bookstore — you won't have a private pension plan. All members of the Canadian workforce, whether employed or self-employed, are entitled to CPP/QPP benefits, so you'll have a modest pension coming in from that source. OAS will supplement this, assuming you don't lose it through the "claw back" system. If you had a comfortable annual income, you'll have private investments, including traditional income-generating investments like stocks, bonds, and term deposits (GICs), of course, as well as assets like real estate that can be used to generate regular income. Much of this may be sheltered in RRSPs — we'll explain later how they work. If you were savvy, disciplined, and lucky, those RRSPs should have grown to considerable size by now. Let's hope so, because income from your RRSP investments is likely to be your primary resource for retirement income.

Maybe you don't fall into either of these categories. Maybe you work in an industry that doesn't offer private pension plans. Maybe you never earned enough to save or invest, or maybe you lost your shirt on technology stocks or income trusts or copper futures. You're likely to find that public pensions are your primary sources of retirement income. Don't despair! In Canada, you can live on the public pension — lots of seniors do. But your options will certainly be more limited than if you had more money. We'll have lots of advice for you on how you might supplement your retirement income.

No matter which of these categories you fall into, with the information in this chapter, you shouldn't have any trouble making an educated estimate about what your retirement income will be. So arm yourself with pen and paper, or a spreadsheet, and start making a running tally. If you have a spouse, you may be wise to carry out this exercise on a family basis, include spousal sources of income as well. By the end of the chapter, you'll be halfway to constructing your Lifestyle Maintenance Budget.

PUBLIC PENSIONS

There are three categories of public benefits payable to older Canadians: Canada Pension Plan (CPP) benefits, payable to all working Canadians who contributed to the plan (if you are a Quebec resident, your pension comes from the Quebec Pension Plan); Old Age Security benefits (OAS), payable to all Canadians over the age of sixty-five, regardless of whether they were members of the workforce or not; and Guaranteed Income Supplement (GIS), paid to the poorest Canadians over the age of sixty-five. We'll discuss each of these benefits individually.

CPP/QPP

How does the plan work?

The Canada Pension Plan (or the Quebec Pension Plan if you reside in Quebec) currently pays a maximum benefit of $863.75 a month (2007). In theory, this amount is designed to replace 25 percent of pre-retirement earnings. In practice, it replaces 25 percent of an average earnings figure, based on a figure known as the Year's Maximum Pensionable Earnings (YMPE), currently set at $43,700 for 2007. Most of these figures are indexed to average wages and salaries; they increase modestly every year.

How much can you personally expect to get in CPP/QPP benefits?

The plan describes itself as a "contributory, earnings-related social insurance program." Every year that you are in the paid workforce and earn over the Minimum Basic Exemption (frozen at $3,500 since 1998), you make a contribution based on your eligible earnings to the CPP, ranging from 1.8 percent when the plan first started in 1966 to 4.95 percent, the current contribution rate. Your employer makes a matching annual contribution on your behalf. If you are self-employed, you contribute the whole amount yourself: currently, it's a total of 9.9 percent of eligible earnings. The pension you will get when you retire is directly related to your personal earnings over the years when you were in the workforce and making contributions.

Individual benefits are calculated according to a formula which takes into account your average annual earnings (up to the YMPE) between the ages of eighteen and sixty-five — a period of forty-seven years. Each of us is entitled to drop from the calculation 15 percent of our contribution time, so the average is based on our best forty years. In addition, parents (but only one parent per child) can drop from the calculation the years when they had children under seven. To be entitled to the maximum benefit, therefore, you would have to have earned and contributed the YMPE for at least forty years (minus any low-earning years when your children were under seven). That's a lot of years, and for many of us, it includes years when we were still in school and earning very little. To date, most retired women are collecting considerably less than the CPP maximum benefit.

The formula is complex and unless you have an obsessive-compulsive streak, you probably haven't been keeping track of your CPP contributions over the years. Fortunately, you don't have to make the calculation yourself. You can find your personal CPP Statement of Contributions on the Internet on the Human Resources and Social Development Canada website (www.hrsdc.gc.ca, click on "individuals" and follow the links to CPP). To view your statement online, you need to apply for a personal access number, which will be mailed to you. With this number, you can keep track of your contribution record as it

Under CPP rules, you can also collect a pension *above* the maximum if you don't claim it at 65 — it increases at the same rate, 0.5 percent per month, for every month between 65 and 70 that you delay taking benefits.

is updated. If you don't like computers, you can ask that the statement be mailed to you once very twelve months.

Should I take my CPP/QPP before I turn 65?

To get the maximum CPP/QPP benefit you need to wait until you are sixty-five before you apply for pension. You are entitled to take your pension as early as age sixty, however, provided you have "wholly or substantially" stopped working (which the plan defines as not earning more than the maximum monthly CPP benefit in the month prior to and the month your pension begins.) The government doesn't care what you earn after that — you could go back to full-time employment a month later, and continue to collect your CPP pension for the rest of your life. If you do that, however, you cannot make further contributions to improve your pension by accumulating more credits.

If you take your CPP/QPP early, you will be penalized in two ways. First of all, the monthly pension payment you would otherwise be entitled to will be reduced by 0.5 percent per month for every month that you are younger than age sixty-five. So the most you could be entitled to if you take a pension at age sixty, assuming you have earned the maximum benefit, is a pension that's 70 percent of the maximum monthly benefit, or $604.62 per month in 2007. In addition, most of us will find that early retirement reduces our average annual earnings. If we got a late start in the workforce or had breaks in service, we won't have anything close to forty years' earnings at the YMPE (maximum pensionable earnings) by the time we reach sixty, and our early retirement pension will be 70 percent of a smaller amount. Some high-earning years between sixty and sixty-five could make an important difference.

Some financial advisors will tell you to wait as long as you can to take your CPP/QPP. After all, it's still a long life after sixty, and if you start out with lower payments, the reduction is permanent — your monthly payments will stay at this level for the rest of your life. But waiting doesn't always make sense, particularly if you expect your income from work to drop sharply after age sixty. The way the benefit formula works, high earning years will bring up the average annual earnings on which your entitlement is calculated, but a number of years with low or no income will bring that average down. If you plan on reducing your work pace after sixty — working part-time, or taking a lower-stress, lower-pay job, for example — you may find that you won't improve your pension substantially by deferring your CPP/QPP benefit by waiting.

If you need the CPP/QPP money for income, by all means take it. That's what it's there for. If you don't need the income right away, and you plan to continue to work and accumulate at least some credits after age sixty, the decision about whether to take your CPP early is more difficult. If you start pension payments early, the actuaries tell us that you'll be ahead if you die before age seventy-eight. If you wait until you're sixty-five to start receiving your pension, you're making a bet that you'll live past age seventy-eight. You can't, of course, predict how long you are going to live. So one strategy is to take the pension benefits early and if you don't need the money right away, invest it and the monies you might otherwise have contributed to CPP, if you're still earning. Then you'll have investment income to add to your income "pot." This will postpone your regret that you claimed early for at least a few more years beyond age seventy-eight.

There is an additional reason some of you may want to take some of your CPP/QPP early and keep your benefits down permanently after age sixty-five. As you will see when we discuss the Old Age Security benefit, it is subject to "claw back" for pensioners with taxable incomes higher than $63,511 in 2007. It would be very poor planning to forgo extra income between ages sixty and sixty-five in order to bump up your CPP/QPP pension payments, only to discover that these higher payments push you into an income bracket from which the extra income simply gets clawed back.

You'll probably want to add a CPP/QPP benefit at age sixty to the income side of your retirement ledger. And you'll certainly want to add it at age sixty-five.

Spousal benefits

CPP/QPP also looks after the interests of spouses of working Canadians, in three different ways.

First of all, it allows for credit-splitting on marriage breakdown, which means that after a divorce, you will still receive half of your ex-spouse's CPP payments. This is mandatory on request of either spouse. So if you stayed out of the workforce to look after the children while your spouse was racking up CPP/QPP credits, and now find yourself alone, you can improve your own pension by forcing him to share those credits.

Second, you can apply to share benefits with your spouse. In simple terms, this means that if one spouse is entitled to a bigger CPP/QPP pension, you can pool the two pensions and split them so that you both get equal pension cheques. This doesn't increase the family pension, but it can improve your overall income situation in two ways. It can help reduce taxes, and sometimes even eliminate an OAS or GIS claw-back. It's a valuable perk. The details are somewhat technical, so consult the Human Resources and Social Development Canada website (www.hrsdc.gc.ca; search "Pension sharing") for information if this is part of your plan.

And third, in addition to the basic pension, the CPP/QPP pays a pension to a surviving spouse. The maximum any Canadian can receive from the plan is $863.75 a month (2007 figures), so if you're lucky enough to be entitled to a maximum CPP benefit based on your own credits, you will get nothing as a spousal pension. But if, like most Canadian women, you're personally entitled to less than the maximum, the spousal pension can "top up" your benefit to the maximum.

Monica Townson, Canada's leading authority on pensions for women, describes the CPP/QPP as a women-friendly pension program. Here are her reasons:

- it applies to all sectors of the economy
- it covers part-time and self-employed workers, not just full-time employees
- it's portable — it follows you if you change jobs
- it doesn't penalize you if you quit work to bear or care for children
- it allows you to share your spouse's benefits on marriage breakdown
- it allows you to share your spouse's benefits on retirement
- it's indexed
- it recognizes a flexible retirement age — anywhere between sixty and seventy
- it provides you with a pension if your spouse dies
- it provides a benefit to dependent children whose parents die

Monica Townson, *Independent Means: A Canadian Woman's Guide to Pensions and Secure Financial Future*, Toronto: MacMillan Canada, 1997

Old Age Security (OAS)

All Canadians, whether or not they have ever been part of the paid work-force, are entitled to the Old Age Security benefit at age sixty-five. Don't forget to apply for it, though — it doesn't come automatically. In 2007, OAS paid a monthly benefit of $491.93.

Unlike CPP/QPP, however, you only get to keep the OAS benefit if the government thinks that you need it. Every Canadian over sixty-five gets a monthly OAS payment — in that sense, it's a universal benefit, but it will be "clawed back" — taxed back — if your income is higher than a certain fixed amount. The mechanism for this claw-back is the income tax system. When you fill out your annual income tax return, you'll have to declare your OAS benefit as part of your taxable income. If your taxable income exceeds the annual claw-back minimum ($63,511 in 2007), you will be charged a surtax of fifteen cents per dollar until you reach the claw-back maximum ($102,865 in 2007). At that point, the amount of the surtax equals the amount of the OAS; in other words, you'll get a tax bill equivalent to the total amount of OAS you received.

This is a somewhat cumbersome system. And the claw-back has come as a shock to more than one senior who has sold the family jewels or the family cottage, triggering a one-time capital gain that puts her over the claw-back limit. But it beats other systems that require seniors to apply for the benefit and pass a means test before receiving it. And once you've filed a tax return showing that you're subject to the claw-back, the government will automatically withhold tax from your monthly OAS payment, so it's not as painful at tax time. If your financial situation changes, you can stop the automatic deductions and revert to full pension.

So include the OAS on the income side of your ledger if you do not anticipate that your taxable income will exceed $63,511. Include a proportionately lesser amount if your taxable income will be between $63,511 and $102,865 annually. If your taxable income will be higher than that, leave OAS out of the calculation altogether — it makes life simpler.

The OAS also pays a spousal benefit. Under the original design of the program, it was called the Spousal Allowance and paid to Canadians between sixty and sixty-five whose spouses were in receipt of OAS. Since women in Canada are on average a few years younger than their husbands, the beneficiaries of this allowance were mostly women. The program has since been expanded, and a similar allowance (called the

We have provided 2007 figures for government benefits. CPP rates are adjusted annually based on average wages and salaries. OAS and GIS rates are adjusted quarterly based on the Consumer Price Index. Up-to-date figures are available on the federal government website. Just go to www.hrsdc.gc.ca and do a search for current rates for CPP and OAS.

Allowance for the Survivor) is now payable as well to those between sixty and sixty-five whose spouses have died — needy widows and widowers (legal or common law, including same-sex relationships, thanks to some recent litigation). The divorced get nothing under this program, although statistically speaking the needs of divorced Canadian women in this age group are as great, or greater, than those who get the benefit.

These allowances are anti-poverty benefits, paid only to the needy. Allowances cease when family income reaches $27,600 (2007) for recipients of the spousal allowance, and $20,064 (2007) for recipients of the allowance for survivors.

Guaranteed Income Supplement (GIS)

In addition to OAS, the federal government pays a Guaranteed Income Supplement (GIS) to the poorest Canadians aged sixty-five and over. This is an anti-poverty benefit, and the amount payable is dependent on marital status and annual income. In 2007, those whose annual incomes fell below $14,904 (exclusive of OAS) qualified for the GIS. For instance, if you are a single person sixty-five or over with no CPP benefits and no earned income at all, you would receive the maximum benefit, $620.91 a month for 2007. You would receive this benefit in addition to your basic OAS. If you did have earned or CPP income, and it was (for example) between $10,080 and $10,103.99, your monthly GIS payment would be $200.91. The GIS benefit is reduced by one dollar for every two dollars of additional income you receive (again, exclusive of OAS). Once you reach an annual non-GIS income of $14,904, for a single person, or $35,712 for a couple, the GIS is eliminated altogether. This formula is designed to ensure that these benefits go to seniors who are truly needy. Fortunately, you don't have to make these calculations yourself. The government has provided a handy on-line calculator that will help you figure out what benefits you and your spouse are eligible for, including GIS, and how they will be affected by increases or decreases in your income. Go to the website for Human Resources and Social Development Canada (www. hrsdc.gc.ca) and search for the Table of Rates for Old Age Security, Guaranteed Income Supplement and Allowance. Let the calculator do the work.

Even if you've been in the workforce and will be entitled to CPP/QPP, you may still qualify for the GIS. If you think you will, include it in your projected retirement income. Just remember to apply for it when the time comes. It doesn't come automatically. Lots of people who qualify for it don't apply for it. And the government doesn't chase them.

PRIVATE PENSIONS
Are You Lucky Enough to Have One?
Approximately one-third of women in the Canadian labor force are members of private pension plans. This percentage has been rising over the last twenty years or so. Unfortunately, for Canadian workers as a whole the number has been going down fairly dramatically at the same time, as more and more employers close or wind up existing pension plans, and more and more newly created jobs come without a pension. So if you've got a private pension plan, count your blessings. You may be one of a dying breed.

But not all pensions are created equal. Some plans are definitely better than others. Before you enter a pension figure in your retirement income ledger, you need to look closely at your own plan.

> Almost 40 percent of Canadian employees are covered by private pension plans: 39.9 percent of men, and 39.1 percent of women. When the self-employed, the unemployed and those who work in family businesses without wages are factored in, however, the coverage figure drops to 33 percent.
>
> Statistics Canada, *Proportion of labour force and paid workers covered by a registered pension plan (RPP)* (1998-2002)

What Kind of Pension Plan Do You Belong To?

There are two basic types of pension plan. Only one of these, the defined benefit (DB) pension plan, is what most of us think of as a *real* pension. This type of plan pays out a specific monthly benefit payment for life, guaranteed. Plan members can calculate ahead of time exactly how much they will get, and exactly how much that monthly benefit will be improved if they get a raise in their last few years of employment, or put in more years of service. Some of these defined benefit plans are even indexed or partially indexed to inflation, which means that the benefit will increase over the years as the cost of living rises. The defined benefit plan is the gold standard, the kind of pension plan we all wish we had. Teachers, public employees and unionized nurses typically have DB plans.

> You're more likely to have a good private pension if you're unionized. In 1999, the last year for which data is available, almost 80 percent of unionized workers were members of private pension plans; only 27 percent of non-union workers had private pension coverage.
>
> Monica Townson, "The Impact of Precarious Employment on Financial Security in Retirement", in *New Frontiers of Research on Retirement*, Statistics Canada, 2006

Defined contribution (DC) pension plans function more like personal savings accounts or RRSPs (see discussion below). In these plans, the employer puts in a fixed amount of money annually (a "defined contribution") for each employee. That money, together with the employee's own contributions, then gets invested on the employee's behalf: sometimes as part of an investment pool, but more often by the employee herself, based on a menu of investment choices offered by the plan. When the employee retires, the money in her investment account is used to purchase an investment product that will produce retirement income. Annuities are a popular choice among retirees who want a guaranteed monthly income (see RRSPs, below, for a discussion of how annuities work).

DB plans were the norm in the heyday of private pensions — in the years when the Post-War Retirees were retiring. These plans all functioned in more or less the same way — employers contributed enough money to the plan to build up a fund that could pay out pensions to retirees at the levels guaranteed by the plan. Sometimes employees contributed as well, but in many cases the plan was solely funded by the employer. This wasn't a heavy burden in years when the stock market was booming — big investment returns meant that the pension fund often generated enough revenue in a year to fully fund the plan and pay out the benefits without requiring any contributions at all from the employer. In those years, employers took what is called "contribution holidays." When the plans produced really big surpluses, employers could even take money out of the plan if they followed the rules.

But pension surpluses are fast becoming a thing of the past. Pension investment funds haven't done well lately, and changes to actuarial rules have transmuted many pension surpluses into deficits. Worldwide, employers are converting existing DB plans to DC plans. This trend has been slower to gain momentum in Canada than it has south of the border, but it's likely coming, and very few new DB plans are being created. Employers like DC plans because they don't like uncertainty. They've figured out that while DB plans are great in the good times, in the bad times they may have to dip into profits to fund substantial pension plan deficits. DC plans allow employers to predict and budget for their annual costs, and in these days of economic change and uncertainty, most employers see predictability as just better business. Hence the trend to DC plans.

But from a pension plan member's point of view, the downside is obvious. DC plans remove pension risk from employers simply by shifting that risk to employees. Once the employers have made their required contribution for each employee every year, they are off the hook. They don't have to worry about what happens to the money. In DC plans, employees usually manage their own individual pension accounts, making their own investment decisions. This means — let's face it — that pension investments in these plans are being managed by amateurs rather than professionals.

And the amount of monthly income that comes out the other end will depend on how generous an annuity you can buy with your retirement funds. And that will depend, when all is said and done, on two things over which you, the employee, will have little or no control: investments returns during the life of the plan, and interest rates on your date of retirement. These factors are difficult to predict, and employees with defined contribution pension plans can't calculate their pensions in advance with any degree of certainty. An individual plan member can only speculate about what pension she will receive when she retires, and how much difference a salary increase or more years of service will make to her future retirement income. Planning becomes more difficult.

But with all its deficiencies, a DC pension is a whole lot better than no private pension at all. If you have one, count yourself lucky. You can add a significant dollar figure to the prospective income side of your retirement ledger, even if you can't calculate with precision exactly what that amount will be.

To determine what figure you should use for planning purposes,

GROUP RRSPs

Some employers sponsor group RRSPs instead of pension plans. A group RRSP is really nothing more than an administrative mechanism which operates as an umbrella for a number of individual RRSPs. Group RRSPs are not regulated like pension plans, and do not promise to pay specific benefits. If you are part of group RRSP plan, see the section on RRSPs, below, for an explanation of how your benefits will produce retirement income.

you can go to one of a number of good calculators available on the Internet that will help you figure out how money increases in value over time, and how to convert lump sums into monthly income. This calculation will be done in the same way for DC balances and for RRSP lump sums, and will be discussed in more detail in the RRSP section below.

Spousal Private Pensions

Even if you don't have a pension yourself, if your spouse has one you have certain rights to that pension, protected by law. It is now the rule in Canada that every pension plan must offer a "joint and survivor pension." This means that when the pensioner dies, the spouse will continue to receive payments from the pension plan.

The catch, though, is that these rights can be waived. If both the pension plan member and his/her eligible spouse sign a waiver of spousal benefits prior to the commencement of pension payments, the plan can pay out a pension to the member alone, and the spouse will get nothing when the member dies. The inducement to waive spousal benefits is usually a larger monthly pension payable to the spouse alone. It's always dangerous to hand out general advice, and everybody's personal situation is different. But it's fair to say that there are very few situations in which waiving the right to a spousal pension would benefit the spouse. So if you're asked to sign one of these waivers, get financial and legal advice before you do so. It could be a costly decision.

In most Canadian provinces, a surviving spouse is automatically entitled by law to a pension equal to at least 60 percent of the amount received by the pensioner, unless she has waived the benefit. Some pension plans allow an even better joint and survivor pension, up to 100 percent. There's a price for this, of course: the more generous the pension allocated to a surviving spouse, the lower the basic pension payment during the lifetime of the pensioner. On a monthly basis the reduction is surprisingly modest, however, and most couples feel that the lower payments are worth it in order to ensure that both of them can count on reasonable pension income for the rest of their lives.

WILL MY PENSION STILL BE THERE WHEN I NEED IT?

If you read the newspapers, you know that there is much hysteria south of the border these days about whether Social Security pensions (the U.S. equivalent of both the OAS and the CPP/QPP) will actually be there when our American sisters retire. We hear that the American Social Security system is grossly underfunded, and will soon be bankrupt. The Bush administration whipped up much of this hysteria in support of its proposal to privatize social security, diverting a portion of employer and employee contributions into private investment accounts, and letting those investment geniuses who frequent your office cafeteria or local watering hole take care of their own retirement security.

Many pension experts think that privatizing public pension benefits is a very bad idea. They argue that public pension plans don't need to be pre-funded in the same way that private plans do, and that "reform" (privatization) will benefit no one except the financial services industry, which stands to make huge dollars managing those millions of private retirement accounts. While it would be rash to predict the final outcome of the U.S. debate, at the moment it looks like the privatizers are losing the battle and social security will go unreformed for a few more years.

Fortunately, Canadians do not have to leap into this debate at all, thanks to a series of reforms culminating in 1998 that increased contribution levels for both employers and employees. Our Canada Pension Plan is secure, and your CPP/QPP benefit will be there when you need it.

Can the same be said for your private retirement pension? If you've been paying attention to the business news lately, you'll have noticed that many pension plans, including some very big plans sponsored by important companies, are reporting deficits. Even the erstwhile invincible

Ontario Teachers' Pension Plan has reported deficits. What does this all mean? How safe are Canadian private pension plans? If you belong to a pension plan, can you count on that money to be there when you retire? And what about twenty years after you've left the work force and nobody remembers your name any more?

The good news is that Canada has a pretty impressive regulatory system for pensions. Government agencies monitor pension funds for solvency on a regular basis, and require employers to keep their contributions up-to-date. A solvent company doesn't have a choice about maintaining a solvent pension fund — it's the law! Ups and downs in the investment market may mean that when a financial snapshot is taken at any given moment, there may not be enough money in the plan to pay all the benefits the plan will ever be called upon to pay. But as long as the company stays in business that's not a serious practical problem. The plan won't ever have to pay out all of the benefits at once. The markets will recover, and the company will rebalance the books over time — in most Canadian jurisdictions a company has five years to rebalance. Pensioners rarely suffer from these temporary solvency deficiencies.

But what if the company doesn't recover, and doesn't stay in business? The bad news is that from time to time a pension plan does become really insolvent. This only happens if the plan is seriously in deficit and the company then goes bankrupt. You can't get blood out of a stone, and if your employer is broke, the pension fund may find itself in the middle of a long line of unlucky creditors who will not be paid. Even then, though, the money that's already in the pension fund can't be touched by the employer or any other creditors. At worst, you may see some reduction — usually a modest one — in your benefits. In Ontario, there's a government guarantee backing up at least minimum pension payments in the unlikely event that your plan hits the rocks.

So you should certainly count on your pension plan in your retirement planning. It's as solid as anything else in this uncertain world.

RRSPs
What Are RRSPs, and How Do They Work?

RRSP is the ubiquitous acronym for Registered Retirement Savings Plan. We've had RRSPs in Canada since 1957. We've all heard of them and many of us own them, but not all of us understand how they work.

An RRSP is a construct of the income tax system, primarily directed at workers who do not have private pension plans. RRSPs replicate some of the tax advantages enjoyed by pension plans — contributions to RRSPs are tax deductible and the funds accumulate interest, dividends, and capital gains on a tax-free basis until they are withdrawn. In other words, RRSPs are simply tax shelters promoted by the government in order to assist Canadians to save for retirement.

Contrary to popular belief, an RRSP is not a specific investment. It's just a tax-sheltered account. You can set up a very simple RRSP by buying a tax-sheltered, off-the-shelf GIC from a financial institution like a bank or credit union. Or you can open an investment account, called a self-directed RRSP, in which you can tax-shelter eligible investments. Up until 2005, there were limits on foreign investments in RRSPs, but those limits have now been removed. So you can make almost any standard investment available on the market within your RRSP: term deposits, mutual funds, equities, bonds, mortgages, income trusts, almost anything that can be valued. It's your money, and you can invest it as you see fit.

The amount of money you can accumulate in your RRSP depends on a number of factors. First and foremost is the issue of how much you can contribute to your RRSP in any given tax year. There is a general annual ceiling for RRSP contributions: $19,000 for 2007, and $20,000 for 2008. But that's a maximum, and not every taxpayer is permitted to contribute that much. You may not earn enough to reach the maximum. The formula caps your individual contribution at 18 percent of your earned income in the previous tax year. In addition, if you or your employer has made a contribution to a registered pension plan on your behalf (this figure is called your "pension adjustment" or PA) in any given year, that amount will be deducted from your 18 percent limit.

Not everybody wants, or can afford, to use up all her contribution room. But let's assume that you have followed the advice so bountifully bestowed upon you by the financial services industry every January and February, and contributed the maximum every year. There are a number of additional factors that will affect how much money will accumulate in your RRSP by the time you retire.

There is the question of how you choose to invest your contributions. You can invest your RRSP contributions wisely or unwisely, luckily or unluckily. You can make safe investments or high risk investments, good investments or bad investments. Based on the general financial advice that's out there, you'll probably aspire to earn somewhere between 6 and 8 percent on your RRSP. You can take comfort from statistics: Canadian equities, we are told, have produced average returns of around 12 percent per year over the last thirty years, and bonds, with less risk, have averaged around 8 percent. These figures are useful for planning purposes. But averages conceal dramatic fluctuations. You can't guarantee your own investment choices will do anything like this well. You can lose your shirt within your RRSP, just like you can with any other investment, if you're not careful.

There is also the issue of how long your money stays in your plan: whether you leave it there until the government makes you take it out (currently at age sixty-nine, although the March 2007 federal budget proposes to increase this age to seventy-one), or whether you withdraw it earlier. The RRSP tax rules do not require you to leave the money in until you need it for retirement; they simply provide that when you withdraw it, you have to pay income tax on it. For most people with jobs, the prospect of a substantial tax hit is disincentive enough to leave their RRSP money alone and look to other resources to cover short-term cash needs. But sometimes people collapse their RRSPs during periods of unemployment, including maternity leave, since money withdrawn when no other income is being earned will usually be taxed at a lower rate. While this might appear to be a good short-term fix, it's very poor retirement planning. You will never be able to make up for either the RRSP contribution room squandered in this way, or the tax-free accumulation time you've lost.

Immediate financial need is not the only pressure on Canadians to withdraw money from their RRSPs for purposes other than retirement income. In recent years the government has positively invited people to raid their RRSPs through two programs, the Home Buyers Plan and the Lifelong Learning Plan, which allow Canadians to withdraw RRSP money and use it towards the purchase of a new home or to pursue full-time post-secondary education or training. These are worthy goals, and the temptation may be irresistible, but remember that taking your money out early can wreak havoc on your retirement planning. Under both these programs you don't pay any immediate tax penalty, and you are required to put the money back into your plan over time (ten to fifteen years), so you don't lose the contribution room in your RRSP. (If you don't repay on schedule, you'll have to pay tax on the money you withdrew.) But you do lose many years of tax-free accumulation on the money, which can subtract many thousands of dollars from your nest egg. Make sure you've carefully explored all other sources of money for home buying or further education before you "borrow" from your RRSP.

Spousal RRSPs

Spousal RRSPs are retirement income-splitting devices. They allow a higher income spouse with a substantial RRSP and/or private pension to use his or her RRSP contribution room to build up a retirement fund for a lower income spouse. When it comes time to withdraw the money from the fund, it's taxed to the lower income spouse. The family saves tax overall. Instead of one large retirement income coming in, there will be two smaller incomes, and they'll be taxed at lower rates.

A spousal RRSP may be a good idea for you and your partner if you have a substantial income disparity now, or anticipate one in retirement, perhaps because one of you has a private pension plan and one of you doesn't. It's not too late to set one up now, if you haven't already done so — even if you've only got a few more years before you have to cash out your plans, every little bit of income splitting helps with the tax bill down the road.

The federal government has recently announced a change to the income tax rules that would allow couples to split pension income, including income from RRSPs, without going through the mechanics of setting up a spousal RRSP. Some commentators have suggested that if this tax change goes through — and as this book goes to press, it's not law yet — spousal RRSPs will become obsolete. It's true that they won't be as useful. But you may still want to consider setting one up, and if you've already got one, you certainly shouldn't collapse it without getting some advice. One key reason is that the proposed federal plan permits splitting RRSP income only after age sixty-five; a spousal RRSP would allow you the benefit of income splitting at any time, so it may still save some tax for those contemplating early retirement.

How Will I Turn My RRSP Into Retirement Income?

Remember that an RRSP is just a tax shelter. It's your money. It's not locked in, and you can take it out, in whole or in part, any time you want to as long as you're prepared to pay the tax on it, and forgo the benefit of future tax-sheltered accumulation. But the system is designed to reward those who don't take it out until they need it for retirement.

When you do decide to take it out (which by law must be done at age sixty-nine, or seventy-one if the March 2007 federal budget proposals are implemented), you have some choices about what to do with it:

- You can simply cash it in
- You can buy an annuity
- You can convert it into a RRIF (Registered Retirement Income Fund)

If you simply cash it in, you'll get hit with a large tax bill, since every penny of it will be taxable in one year. If your RRSP is a significant amount, this will leave you with much less money to fund your retirement and largely defeat the purpose for which you saved in the first place. In order to avoid that result, the government offers the other two options. These are special investment mechanisms that allow you to turn your lump sum RRSP into a retirement income stream that will be paid out over time, and taxed only when you receive it, usually at a lower rate.

Annuities

An annuity is a contract you make with a financial institution. You turn over your lump sum, permanently, and in return the financial institution agrees to pay you an annual income. Annuities are a type of insurance contract, and like any other insurance contract, their cost will depend on factors like your age and gender at the time you make the purchase. Cost will also depend a great deal on interest rates at the time you make the purchase, because at least theoretically, the financial institution will be paying your annuity out of the investment proceeds of the money you've paid for the annuity.

The standard annuity is an agreement to pay an income for life. There are many other options, of course: "term certain" annuities that

For an Internet calculator that allows you to check out monthly annuity payments for annuities purchased at various ages and for various capital amounts, check out www.totalreturnannuities.com. We certainly don't advise purchasing annuities online, but this is useful planning information for projecting your retirement income.

cease at a specific age; "joint and last survivor" annuities that make payment to a couple for both their lifetimes; annuities for life, but with a guarantee period (e.g. ten years) providing that payments will continue to be made for that length of time, even if the annuitant dies before the guarantee expires. All of these wrinkles come with an additional cost, of course, which means that for the same capital investment, your monthly annuity payments will be lower.

RRIFs

A RRIF operates somewhat differently than an annuity. It works more like an RRSP, in the sense that your money remains your money, invested as you see fit within the confines of the tax-sheltering RRIF. The major difference between a RRIF and an RRSP is that you can't just leave your money in a RRIF to grow indefinitely. You *must* set up an annual schedule of withdrawals. The older you are, the higher the annual amount you must withdraw. Under prior rules, the schedule of payments had to ensure that your RRIF balance would be reduced to zero by the time you turned eighty-five. With higher life expectancies, that requirement is now gone, but the basic objective remains the same — to ensure that you take the money out to live on. The compulsory withdrawal system creates some risk that you'll outlive your RRIF assets, so you'd be well advised to tuck some savings away out of your RRIF withdrawals if you can afford it, to provide for this possibility.

You can convert your RRSP to a RRIF anytime you want to; you can do it right now if you want to. But it's best to wait until you absolutely have to. Because once you convert to a RRIF and begin to make withdrawals, you can't stop. If you really need a steady stream of retirement income right now, that works fine. But if you just need a lump sum to tide you over a rough spot, it's far better just to make a partial withdrawal and leave the rest in the RRSP until you're sixty-nine (or seventy-one if the March 2007 federal budget proposals become law).

If you like to be in control of your money and you're a good (or a lucky) investor, you'll probably do better overall with a RRIF than with an annuity. But there are no guarantees — you might do a lot worse. When it comes time to make the choice, be sure to seek advice about which choice is best for your personal circumstances.

Meanwhile, if you've got RRSPs, make an entry in your retirement income ledger. Unless you go out and buy an annuity right now, you'll have to estimate the size of the entry. But for now, you can use an Internet annuity calculator to determine the approximate annual income your lump sum will generate. The rule of 4 percent, used by many conservative financial planners, will also give you a rough guide. Assume that you will draw out no more than 4 percent of your lump sum each year; if you're aiming for $1,000,000 in your RRSP by the time you retire, the rule of 4 percent would net you an annual income of $40,000.

INTERNET RETIREMENT PLANNING CALCULATORS

Identifying your potential sources of retirement income, and trying to figure out how much each of them will yield isn't easy. It's tempting to look for some shortcuts, especially if your math skills aren't strong.

Try Googling the phrase "retirement planning calculators." You'll be greeted by literally hundred of websites offering to help you figure out how much money you will need for your retirement. Many of these websites, especially those sponsored by banks, brokerage houses or insurance companies, invite you to enter your data into online mini-programs that will do your calculations for you. How useful are these retirement calculators in helping you focus on sources of retirement income?

Most calculators operate on the same basic principle. You enter the age at which you expect to retire, your life expectancy after retirement, your target retirement income, and your expected financial resources. The program then performs a calculation to determine whether you have enough money to meet your income goals. Then, because you almost certainly *don't* have enough, it goes on to tell you how much money you will have to save before retirement in order to generate the income you need to maintain your desired standard of living. And, *of course*, because they're in the business, they'll be happy to sell you investment products to buy with your retirement savings, products that will speed you on your way to the retirement of your dreams.

One frustrating shortcoming of these calculation programs is that they require *you*, the potential retiree, to provide most of the information critical to the calculation. You are asked to specify the age you want to retire — fair enough. But after that it gets harder. *How long to you expect to receive retirement income?* In other words, how long do you intend to live? *What percentage of your current income will you need for retirement?* You may have no idea. (In Chapter 5, we'll try to help with that question.) *What do you expect the average rate of inflation to be during your retirement?* Even the Governor of the Bank of Canada probably skips that question! *What rate of return do you expect to receive on your investments?* Hope springs eternal, but who really knows?

It doesn't take long to figure out that the information generated by most of these calculators is pretty meaningless. Even the experts are only speculating when they try to predict inflation rates and investment returns. While it is prudent to plan on the basis of at least average life expectancy, you might die the day after you retire, ensuring that your retirement savings will long outlast you. Or you might be one of those statistical anomalies who lives to a venerable and vigorous 100, while the retirement planning calculator expects you to die at eighty-five.

Some of these calculators are more useful than others, providing default settings that give you the benefit of expert consensus on such esoteric matters as projected rates of inflation, or at least enough basic background information about historical data and expert projections to make your guesses more realistic. Some of them take into account government pensions and benefits (a surprising number of them, inexplicably, do not!). Some of them prompt users for input on other sources of retirement income, such as part-time work or non-registered investments. The best of them provide supplementary calculators that will allow you to translate lump sum non-registered investments into annuity values that can then become part of your projected retirement income. We've listed some good ones below.

- **Fiscal Agents**
  www.fiscalagents.com
  Look under "Financial Tools." A well-designed and user-friendly calculator, which prompts you for information, and allows you to change variables with ease. Provides a detailed, useful, and printable report.

- **Human Resources Development Canada**
  https://srv260.hrdc-drhc.gc.ca
  Focuses on government benefits and private pensions. Reliable and easy to use.

- **Retirement Advisor**
  www.retirementadvisor.ca
  Look under "Tools." Provides information in the form of useful, readable charts and graphs.

- **seclonLogic**
  www.seclonlogic.com
  This website offers a comprehensive and easy to use retirement planning calculator. It also offers a tool which allows you to calculate how much annual income a lump sum will produce, and compares outcomes for annuities and RRIFs.

THE ROLE OF THE PROFESSIONAL FINANCIAL PLANNER

We haven't said much up to this point about professional financial planners. There are lots of them about these days. Should you hire one? Would expert advice help you to determine where to find enough income for a comfortable retirement? Perhaps. But not as much as you might think.

A competent and experienced financial planner can provide a useful perspective by:

* making sure that you take account of government sources of income

* drawing your attention to the impact of tax breaks for seniors and government health care benefits

* helping you understand the impact of inflation on both your investments and your income needs

* helping you identify what expenses typically increase or decrease after retirement, and by how much

* advising on tax-effective ways of investing and harvesting your retirement income: e.g should you cash in your RRSP right away, or spend your non-registered investments first? should you take your CPP at age sixty, or wait until you are sixty-five? what investment strategies might best protect you from the OAS claw-back?

* advising on planning and investing strategies for leaving an estate to your children

* recognizing gaps in your planning, and providing advice on how to fill them.

But beware! Not all financial planners see their job as helping you live within your income. Financial planners work in the financial services industry, even if they don't work directly for banks or insurance companies or brokerage houses. (Many of them do, of course — and here we thought they were working for us!) And that means that many financial planners know far more about investments than they do about retirement.

Read this book carefully before you go to see a financial planner. You'll be better equipped to ask the right questions. And you may find when you get there that you know more about retirement income and expenses than the planner does!

CHAPTER 5
Projecting Retirement Expenses

HOW MUCH IS ENOUGH?

By now you should have a rough but useful idea of how much retirement income you can plan for. Will this be enough to ensure a comfortable retirement?

The conventional wisdom is that we need 70 percent of our pre-retirement income to finance a comfortable retirement. Many online retirement planning calculators use 70 percent as their default target income. Many financial advisors give the same advice. But the reality out there is that most retired Canadians *don't* replace 70 percent of their pre-retirement income. Studies show that, in fact, only the poorest Canadians do. If you earn less than $10,000 annually, you'll actually do better when you retire than you did when you were working. Government benefits will replace some 115 percent of your income (as you'll see in the table, next page). But as pre-retirement income rises, the percentage of income Canadians are able to replace after retirement falls. Canadians who earn over $70,000 replace, on average, about 53 percent of their income. Middle-income Canadians may *aspire* to replace 70 percent of their income, but they are obviously surviving on a lot less, many of them quite comfortably.

Retirement Income as a Percentage of Pre-Retirement Income for Canadians

Pre-Retirement Income	Men	Women
Under $10,000	217%	115%
$10,000 to $20,000	75%	65%
$20,000 to $30,000	64%	59%
$30,000 to $40,000	60%	60%
$40,000 to $50,000	59%	58%
$50,000 to $70,000	56%	56%
Over $70,000	44%	48%

From Table 5 of *Factors Affecting the Economic Status of Older Women in Canada: Implications for Mandatory Retirement*, a study prepared for the British Columbia Human Rights Commission by Arlene Tigar McLaren and Margaret Menton Manery in 2000.

The 70 percent figure is far from scientific. It's based on certain standard assumptions about what your life looks like now. For example, it assumes that

- your current income is sufficient to pay your current expenses;
- you're currently making payments on a mortgage that will be paid off when you retire;
- you're still raising your children, but you're doing such a good job that they'll be fully self-sufficient after you retire.

It's also based on certain standard assumptions about what your retirement will look like. For example, it assumes that

- when you retire, you'll leave the workplace — for good;
- after you retire, you'll have no more income from work;
- because you're not working any more, you won't have any more work-related expenses;

- since you won't retire until you have a big enough nest egg, you won't need to save for retirement any more.

Above all, it's based on assumptions about the retirement lifestyle to which you aspire. In particular, it assumes that after retirement, your principal objective will be to maintain your current lifestyle.

But what if those assumptions don't describe your life or your retirement aspirations? Maybe the very first assumption, that your current income is adequate for your needs, doesn't fit the facts. Many Canadian women live right on the edge, barely able to keep up with their current expenses while they're still employed. They'll carry a mortgage and other debts into retirement. For this group of women, 70 percent of pre-retirement income may be less than enough. They may need 100 percent, every cent they've currently got coming in, to maintain their pre-retirement lifestyle. For others — the lucky ones — current income is more than enough for their needs. They've been tucking a substantial surplus away for a rainy day, or donating it to charity. They may be able to maintain their current lifestyle on 40 to 50 percent of pre-retirement income, or even less. Still others may have retirement aspirations that include pursuits and ambitions radically different from their current activities. The cost of changing their lives may be quite unrelated to their current cost of living — lower, perhaps, but maybe higher as well.

And to add to the uncertainties, we need to plan for a thirty-year period, a vast span of time in which we can expect that our needs will change — as will the world, the social context within which those needs must be met. No wonder projecting post-retirement income needs feels a lot like shooting at a moving target.

But despite the difficulties and uncertainties, you're embarking on a brand new phase of life, and to make the most of its possibilities, you need to plan. If you don't plan, you won't be able to identify your real options. Is it realistic for you to consider leaving the workforce at age fifty-five? Sixty? Sixty-five? Ever? What will it take for you to stay in your current home as long as you want to? Keep the family cottage? Travel? Maintain your symphony subscription? Contribute to your grandchildren's education? If you think things through and plan realistically, you'll know whether working longer is a necessity or simply an option for you. You'll know whether your dream of downsizing to a waterfront penthouse in Toronto is attainable. Maybe that's not realistic; maybe a double-wide south of Winnipeg is more likely to be your retirement home. But you'll know. You'll be out there, in new territory, but you'll have a map and a compass.

For planning purposes, let's start by pretending that the traditional retirement assumptions still describe you and your situation. We'll assume that once you retire, you're planning to be out of the workplace for good. We'll also assume that at the moment, you are still working, and your planning objective is to maintain your current lifestyle. Based on those assumptions, we'll put together the information you need, the questions you need to ask yourself, and the factors that will determine your income needs when you aren't working for pay any more. We'll help you take a snapshot of how much it costs to do that right now, and then we'll help you figure out how much income it will take to maintain that lifestyle when your paycheck stops coming.

GETTING A FOCUS ON CURRENT SPENDING

The problem with the 70 percent rule used by the financial planners is that it focuses on income. Projecting expenses based on income is not a very helpful or realistic approach to budgeting. It's looking through the wrong end of the telescope. What we should be looking at for guidance isn't *current income*. It's *current spending*. That's what defines your lifestyle. Let's look at how you spend your money right now. And then let's look closely and critically at how those spending patterns might alter when you retire. So sit down, focus on the here and now, and figure out where your money goes.

There's no substitute for preparing a budget. If you don't know what your current spending categories are, and how much you spend on each one, you've got some homework to do before you can start to project retirement income needs. Be realistic. For example, if you're living with someone else as part of an economic unit — if you're a family — don't budget as if you weren't. You'll have to account for your total household expenses. In return, of course, you'll get to consider your total household income.

Here's a detailed list of household budget categories. It's detailed for a reason — it's the small items that get away from us when we're planning, and the small items can really add up. Note the budget categories that apply to you. Disregard the ones that don't, and add any that are unique to you and your family. Maybe your dog and cat have special medical expenses, or you and your husband always travel to see solar eclipses wherever they occur. This is a very personal snapshot of your spending, so make sure it really reflects you and your family, if you have one.

SPENDING CATEGORIES	MONTHLY	YEARLY
Accommodation:		
Rent or Mortgage		
Insurance		
Property Taxes		
Cleaning		
Garden		
Maintenance		
Miscellaneous		
Groceries		
Auto:		
Fuel		
Insurance		

License Fees		
Parking		
Maintenance		
Public Transit		
Utilities:		
Electric		
Heating		
Telephone (incl. Cell)		
Internet		
TV Access		
Water & Sewage		
Subscriptions		
Clothing		
Medical (incl. insurance premiums)		
Fitness		
Personal Care		
Recreation:		
Dining Out		
Theater & Movies		
Books		
Music		
Vacations		
Gifts		
Donations		
Income Tax		
Dry Cleaning		
Computer		
Tuition Fees		

Life Insurance		
Personal Savings		
TOTAL		

Once you've got your personal budget categories identified, you need to track how much you spend on each one of these items. For utilities, get out your old bills, your checkbook, or your bank statement and figure out how much you spent last year. For items like groceries and dry cleaning, you'll find it easier to track spending if you've paid by debit or credit card; if you haven't, you may have to track ahead for a month or two and record expenditures. For "petty cash" items like your daily latte and muffin, there's no substitute for writing down your spending every single day. You don't have to do this for the rest of your life — just long enough to be sure that you've captured your typical spending patterns and can project them into an annual budget.

BUDGETING FOR POST-RETIREMENT LIVING

After you've done the calculations and you know what it's really costing you to live *before* you retire, it's time to look at what it will cost you to live *after* you retire. Which of your spending categories will remain constant after you retire? Are there categories that will go up? By how much? Think hard. Be creative, but be conservative. *And don't cheat!*

We've all heard the conventional wisdom that retirement living is less expensive. There are usually savings that flow simply from not working any more, often substantial savings. We're not talking here about "cutting back" or pinching pennies. We're talking about the savings you'll

There are lots of free budget worksheets on the Internet. Check out www.banking.pcfinancial.ca, (click on "Helpful Stuff", then "Tools and Calculators"). Industry Canada's Office of Consumer Affairs also has a number of useful online tools to help you track spending. Go first to the Government of Canada's Spending Smarter website, www.strategis.ic.gc.ca, then click on "Consumers," then "Canada's Office of Consumer Affairs". A sidebar menu lists "Tools and Calculators." You can also track household spending and prepare budgets with software programs like Intuit Quicken and Microsoft Money. If you don't like computers or don't have one, there are books that provide budgeting charts and worksheets. Or just get a lined notebook and do it yourself! But do it!

benefit from just because it's cheaper to be not working than it is to be working.

Let's identify some obvious areas in which your expenditure will be reduced simply because you're not working any more. Keep a running total — you'll need these figures later on to put together your Lifestyle Maintenance Budget.

CPP Contributions and EI Premiums

If you're an employee, you may not even know that you've been making contributions to the Canada Pension Plan and paying Employment Insurance premiums. They're deducted from your paycheck by your employer, and remitted to the government on your behalf, so you don't pay them out of your pocket. (Your employer makes matching contributions.) But these costs are very real. And when you retire, you won't have to pay them any more.

If you're self-employed, you haven't paid EI premiums. But you have been paying CPP contributions, out of pocket, through the income tax system. And those CPP contributions are twice as much as they would be if you were an employee, since you pay the matching employer contribution yourself.

These amounts — called statutory remittances — can add up to big numbers. A woman who earns at least $40,000 a year from employment pays the maximum EI premium: $720 in 2007. A woman who earns at least $43,700 a year makes the maximum CPP contribution: $1,989.90 in 2007 for employees, and $3,979.80 if she's self-employed. At these salary levels, you've been paying out between $2,709.90 and $4,699.80 for statutory benefits. This expense will disappear after retirement.

Pension and RRSP Contributions

Once you've stopped working, you won't be making contributions to your company pension plan. And once you've accumulated your retirement nest egg, you won't need to make any more contributions to your RRSP. If these expenses were part of your annual budget, they'll be gone.

Let's assume you were a high enough earner to contribute the legal maximum amount, $19,000 a year for 2007, to a pension plan, an RRSP, or a combination of both. When you stop making those contributions, you'll reduce your annual cash outlay by that amount.

Disability Insurance Premiums

While many employee benefits are funded by employers, disability insurance premiums are often an exception. For income tax reasons, employees frequently pay their own disability premiums. If you were self-employed, and you purchased disability insurance — not everybody does, of course, but it's advisable — you have been paying your own premiums, and they can be fairly hefty. Now that you're retired, you don't need this insurance any more. In fact, you can't use it, since disability insurance only pays out if you earn income and you lose the opportunity to earn that income as a result of a disability.

Disability insurance is expensive. If you were a high income professional, you could well have been paying out in excess of $2,500 a year in disability premiums. Not anymore!

Clothing

No, retirement doesn't eliminate the need for clothing! But if you've had a white-collar job, you can count on your wardrobe costs being much reduced after you leave the workplace. A pair of blue jeans, even designer jeans, will cost a lot less than those three indispensable pinstripe wool-and-cashmere suits you bought last year in black, navy, and taupe. And you can throw those jeans in the washing machine — dry cleaning costs for professional wardrobes can run to hundreds of dollars a year.

For the sake of our notional calculations, assume that you can cut your clothing and dry cleaning costs by 25 percent a year. A substantial saving — let's say $1,000 a year.

Transportation

After retirement, your transportation costs will be less, maybe much less. You won't be driving to work every day, and you can park for nothing at the mall. How much you save on parking will depend on where you live. Calgary has now zipped past Toronto as the most expensive city in Canada for parking. But it could be as much as $200-400 a month. If you and your spouse have both been driving to work, you can also consider getting rid of one of your cars (the choice of who gets to give up the car will be quite painless, of course!). But for now, since you're not modifying your lifestyle yet, you can budget to keep the second car.

The Canadian Automobile Association estimates that it costs the average Canadian between $8,500 and $13,900 a year to own and operate a fairly modest car (we'll look at the cost of running a car in more detail later). It's probably conservative to suggest that in the first year of your retirement, you'll save $2,000 a year on automobile operating costs just because you're not driving to work any more.

Vacation Scheduling

Since we're talking here about maintaining a lifestyle, not changing it, stick to your usual vacation choices for budgeting purposes. If you've got retirement plans to travel the world, you'll have to budget for that separately. Here we're talking about your regular stress-busting trips to the spa, your Caribbean vacation, your European getaway, or your annual package to Las Vegas. But now that you're retired, you no longer need to go places when everybody else does. You can go to the spa mid-week, when the prices are lower. You don't have to book into the resort of your dreams during March break. You don't even have to plan ahead — you can go on a half-price last-minute January special. You can take advantage of lower seasonal fares and fly to Europe in March instead of July. You can still do all the things you used to do, but it won't cost you nearly as much. And here's another bonus — it won't be nearly so crowded!

Let's say you normally budget $5,000 a year for vacations. With a little adjustment to your timing, you can get the same vacation, or an even better vacation, for $4,000 now that you're retired. That's a saving of $1,000 a year.

The "Latte Factor"

Here's a big one that's often overlooked. When you track your daily spending, you'll discover something called the "Latte Factor." (Credit where credit is due — Latte Factor is a registered trademark. The phrase was coined by financial planning guru David Bach, author of the *Finish Rich* series, to describe the disappearance of considerable sums of money in small amounts on small luxuries that we could easily do without. On his website (www.finishrich.com), there's a Latte Factor calculator you can use to figure out what $3, $5 or $7 a day, invested over time, would do for you if you didn't pour it down your throat.)

A significant amount of money just gets frittered away in a daily working routine on small items that make the day go more smoothly. We buy a latte on the way in to work. We go out for lunch instead of bringing healthier and less expensive food from home. To make our working relationships go more smoothly we pick up a couple of rounds at the wine bar on Thursday night after work. We contribute to lottery and raffle tickets, purchase chocolate-covered almonds from the accounting clerk to support her child's daycare center, buy Girl Guide cookies for the lunchroom, put $10 in the envelope that's circulating for the receptionist's baby shower. It adds up. When you really look hard, it could well be costing you as much as $50 a week or more.

You won't be doing that any more. And not doing it will save you hundreds of dollars a year. Let's say $2,000, for symmetry's sake.

Your Savings So Far

OK. You've been keeping a running total of your own potential savings in all these categories. Let's add it all up. If you used our default figures, you've just saved more than $30,000 a year without breaking a sweat. If you had an income of $100,000 before you retired, you can support the same lifestyle now on only about $70,000. Yes — we did notice the coincidence. That's 70 percent. We rigged it, of course, but it wasn't much of a stretch. So 70 percent may have some predictive value. But don't count on it — it's no substitute for doing your own math.

The Impact of Income Tax

Actually, you'll be saving more than $30,000, because of a significant fact of Canadian life — income tax. As we all know, Canadians pay for most of their personal expenses with after-tax dollars. If you're in the highest tax bracket (where taxes range from 48.64 percent in Newfoundland, through 46.41 percent in Ontario to 39 percent in Alberta, Canada's current tax haven) you have to earn almost $2 for every $1 you spend, since the other dollar goes to the government.

So what happens if we reduce our spending? It's simple. For our after-tax expenses, *a penny saved can be almost as much as two pennies earned*. Even in the lowest tax brackets, a penny saved is worth 1.2 after-tax pennies.

Let's look at the impact of this rule on your retirement income needs. Assume again that your income is $100,000 a year. At that income level, you probably pay about $30,000 in income tax, and your marginal tax rate is close to 50 percent, unless you've got a very good accountant. When you did the math, you found that after retirement you could cut your personal expenses by about $30,000 without cutting back at all on your lifestyle. Some of those expenditure cuts will not reduce the income tax you pay, because you didn't pay tax on those amounts anyway; they are tax deductible. Pension contributions, RRSP contributions, and half of your CPP contributions if you were self-employed were all taken out of your income before your income tax was calculated — they are effectively paid from *before-tax* dollars. So a large chunk of your savings simply comes off the top. Let's say that for you these savings totalled $20,000. If you needed an income of $100,000 before retirement, you will now need $80,000.

But what about the other $10,000? The transportation expenses, the disability premiums, the vacations, the clothing, the lattes? Those expenses were paid with *after-tax* dollars. In the highest tax bracket, you have to earn $2 for every $1 you spend. If you can reduce your after-tax spending by $10,000, you can get by with an income that's *$20,000* smaller. You now need only $60,000 or 60 percent of your pre-retirement income, to maintain your lifestyle after retirement. It may sound like voodoo economics, but it isn't!

> I like to pay taxes. With them I buy civilization.
>
> Oliver Wendell Holmes Jr.

Will Some of My Expenses Go Up?

Before you get too excited, however, there are still a couple of issues to consider. It's true that many of your expenses are guaranteed to go down when you stop working, even with no changes to your lifestyle. That's great! But there are some areas in which your expenses might go *up*!

An obvious example is a company car. If your employer provided you with a car, you'll lose it when you retire and you'll have to pay for your own transportation. That's expensive. But don't forget that your company car was a taxable benefit. That means that a significant percentage of the annual value of this perk was treated as personal income, and you paid tax on it. If you drove a Lexus to maintain the company image, and you're now happy with a Corolla, you may find that providing your own transportation isn't really much more expensive in the long run.

Another more common example is medical and dental benefits. Canada's national health insurance system pays for hospitalization and most other medical services, But dental, some medical, and prescription drug costs are not covered. Many workplaces that provide these benefits for employees have traditionally extended them to retirees. Benefits insurance is becoming increasingly expensive, however, and the older we get, the more expensive it becomes. There is an accelerating trend in North America toward eliminating post-retirement medical and dental benefits. This is happening in Canada as well as the U.S. Some workplaces still continue medical and dental benefits for retirees. Others do not. Find out about your own situation (and your spouse's). Find out if your plans will continue to provide benefits after you retire. At what level? For how long? Some plans continue benefits for retirees only to age sixty-five. Some provide reduced benefits to retirees. Only a minority provide full retiree benefits for life.

If your employer doesn't offer medical and dental benefits as part of your retirement package, you'll have to pay your own bills or find your own benefits insurance. Make sure you include these costs in your budget. You may be well advised to seek out private insurance. It's expensive, but it's probably worth it. You can get an idea of what medical insurance will cost you at www.healthquotes.ca, which compares a variety of commercial plans, quotes rates for specific coverage, and will, of course, sell you a plan online as well. You may do better if you belong to a professional association (the Retired Teachers of Ontario (RTO) is one example) that offers benefits insurance to its members at group rates. Expect to have to pay between $85 and $170 a month (single) for a basic plan providing medical, dental, and prescription drug coverage. Don't forget that many provincial government medical schemes provide some additional coverage to those over sixty-five, particularly for prescription drugs. The HealthQuotes website provides links to information on provincial medical plans.

A word to the wise. If you're going to purchase your own retirement medical and dental benefits, you should move quickly as soon as you retire. Some plans — RTO is an example — will put you on their plans without proof of insurability if you apply within a short period of termination of your coverage under another group plan, but if you delay your application, you'll need a medical to qualify for some benefits.

Inflation

We've now gone through the process of projecting retirement expenses. So, do we know now how much income we'll need to pay those expenses in retirement? Unfortunately, we don't have the full answer. Here's the problem. The budget we've constructed will only tell us what those goods and services will cost us today. It won't tell us what they will cost tomorrow, or the next day, or thirty years from now.

How far a dollar will go in retirement depends a lot on the rate of inflation. Over the last thirty years, inflation in Canada has averaged about 4.6 percent a year.

That's a useful planning figure for a retirement that might last thirty years. But during the last thirty years, there was a four-year period — 1978 to 1982 — when inflation averaged more than 10 percent a year. You probably remember those years. Many of us were buying our first houses then, and had mortgages at interest rates in excess of 20 percent, unheard-of today. Averages won't mean very much if those days ever return.

Visit the Bank of Canada website (www.bankofcanada.ca), where you'll find a calculator (look under "Monetary Policy") that shows the impact of inflation rates in Canada since 1914 on the cost of a basket of typical goods and services. The website also included a "future value" calculator that allows you to estimate the future value of a lump sum of money, making various interest rate assumptions.

And even at the average rate of inflation, a basket of goods and services that costs us $100 today will cost $340.21 thirty years from now. We can't really predict how inflation is going to affect us. But in calculating our retirement expenses, we would be wise to build in a significant inflation factor. Costs will go up over time — you can count on it.

Your Lifestyle Maintenance Budget

We've looked at sources of retirement income. We've looked at how much it will cost to maintain your current lifestyle once you've left the workplace for good. You've now got the information you need to construct your Lifestyle Maintenance Budget. Now comes the crucial question. Do you have a match? Will your projected sources of retirement income produce enough money for you to maintain your current lifestyle in retirement?

Maybe you were pleasantly surprised by the answer. Lucky you! More likely, you were shocked and appalled. You're wondering how you'll ever make ends meet. Read on.

We'll get you there in the end!

Spending More Sustainably

CHAPTER 6

BUDGETING AGAIN!

If your Lifestyle Maintenance Budget won't balance, you've got some work ahead of you. Maybe you'll have to make adjustments on both sides of the ledger: income as well as expenditure. But maybe some simple economies will find you the equilibrium you need.

Even if your Lifestyle Maintenance Budget does balance, you should read this chapter. Remember, that budget was simply based on a snapshot of your life as it is now. Your needs and wants will change. The world will change. *You* may change. The day may come when cutting expenses is an important part of your life. This chapter will give you some ideas about how to build on the secure foundation you've established. And even if it isn't absolutely necessary, reducing your expenses could give you more freedom. A few extra dollars put aside could give you the flexibility to add a little luxury to your life from time to time — an unbudgeted trip to the South of France, for example, or a new car before the old one has actually driven down its last mile. Or maybe, with some forethought and ingenuity you could save a *lot* more. Learning how to live on less can give you the financial cushion to experiment with a new business, or buy you out of an unrewarding job a few years early. And less expensive living can often be *simpler* living, freeing up time and energy for the more important things in life. If you're reading this in February, you might find it liberating to consider that if you lived in a condo, you could read Proust in your sunroom instead of shovelling the snow off your double driveway after every blizzard. Saving money buys more freedom, more options for what to do with your time.

A word of warning! If you want to live a lower-cost life to achieve more work-free time, make sure your partner, if you have one, is on board. There is nothing more likely to lead to domestic discord than the discovery that the $2,000 you saved by scraping the fifty-year-old wallpaper off the back bedroom all by yourself got squandered by your beloved on the impulse purchase of a new 42-inch plasma screen TV. A spouse who doesn't "get it" can sabotage a financial escape plan faster than you can say "overdraft." If that happens, and one of you has to go back to work to make up the difference, just make sure it isn't you!

Now, let's look at places where retirees can cut expenses.

REDUCING EXPENSES

When addressing women, it's always difficult to know where to start when we introduce the subject of saving money. We don't want to insult you. Many of us were raised by Depression-era mothers who taught us the basics in our cradles — freeze the stale bread to stuff the turkey, recycle the bows and the wrapping paper. If you already know all about this, then you are way out in front. But we are constantly surprised to run into otherwise savvy women who don't know the ABCs of low-cost living. They've just never thought about it. They couldn't tell you where their money goes. They don't know that house brands are just as good as the heavily advertised and more expensive name brand products they're cloned from. They don't wait for the sales to buy their pantyhose. This chapter is for them.

Transportation

Let's look first at some big ticket items. One of the biggest is a car. They are expensive to buy and expensive to operate. When you're budgeting for transportation, you have to look at both these issues. Consider the following chart. The figures are calculated per kilometre of driving:

Cost of car ownership

Vehicle Type	Deprec.	Fuel	Maint. & Repairs	Lic. & Reg.	Finance Charge	Insurance	Total Cost per KM	Total Annual Owner Cost
Toyota Echo	12 cents	4 cents	3 cents	1 cent	12 cents	9 cents	41 cents	$8,200
Chevy Malibu Maxx	20 cents	7 cents	3 cents	1 cent	21 cents	10 cents	61 cents	$12,109
Dodge Caravan	26 cents	6 cents	3 cents	1 cent	24 cents	9 cents	69 cents	$13,838
BMW 530i	46 cents	8 cents	3 cents	1 cent	54 cents	11 cents	$1.23	$24,532

Information for this chart is taken from the *Globe and Mail*, March 31, 2005, pp.G12-G13.

The numbers speak for themselves. Running even the least expensive of these cars is a big chunk out of a retirement budget. If you need to cut your expenses, car ownership is an obvious item to look at.

When you added up your Lifestyle Maintenance Budget expenses in Chapter 5, you probably budgeted to keep both your cars. Now's the time to take a sober second look at that decision. If your family can manage with just one, you'll save yourself a huge chunk of change.

And while you're at it, here's a radical thought. Do you really need a car at all? If you do, do you need the one you've got, or could you get by with one that's cheaper to buy and cheaper to operate?

But I already own my car, you say! *I don't need to worry about items like depreciation and finance charges!* Wrong! You're budgeting now for the long haul, remember? Your car may be paid for today, but eventually you'll have to replace it. If you don't plan now for replacement costs, you'll be faced with a large capital expenditure down the road without the money to pay for it. There's a compromise, of course. Keep the paid-for BMW now, if you can afford the operating expenses, but budget to replace it with a cheaper make and model.

Most of us have lived all our adult lives with a car in the driveway. We are so dependent on our cars that we are scarcely aware of the many viable alternatives to car ownership.

Public transit

In Canadian cities, most places are accessible by public transit. For those days when the weather or the size of your load or the thought of transferring from the subway to the bus deters you from public transit, there are always taxis — expensive, to be sure, but not compared to the cost of car ownership.

For longer journeys, consider trains and inter-city buses. They run frequently and they usually run on time. They're inexpensive. And there's a bonus — you can rough out your next novel while you're traveling, instead of cursing the idiot who's just cut you off on the expressway for the third time.

Public transit is often less convenient and less accessible in the country. But if you're determined, you can still find it. Or create it — through co-operative arrangements with friends and neighbors.

Renting a car

There will be times, of course, when your destination is so obscure or the stuff you have to transport so awkward that a car is the only thing that makes sense. That's what car rental agencies are for. If you think renting is too expensive, look back at our Cost of Car Ownership chart. You could rent an economy car from a reputable agency *every day of the year* for the cost of owning that Dodge Caravan, not to mention the BMW.

Sharing a car

If you co-own a car with another family, you could cut the cost of car ownership by half. Lots of people make informal arrangements to do this, and find it both efficient and cost-effective. It works especially well for those who don't have to go to work every day and can make more flexible use of their time — people like you, when you retire.

Sharing a car is such a good idea that there are now businesses to meet the demand. An idea that started in Europe, auto-sharing has now spread to more than twenty Canadian cities. To see if your city is one of them, check www.carsharing.ca. The concept is simple. In Toronto, for example, a company called AutoShare (www.autoshare.com) owns a fleet of vehicles to which members have access. Members pay an initial membership fee. The basic plan charges a $25 annual administration fee. You then pay for usage. Higher-end plans for higher-volume drivers charge a monthly "retainer" fee plus a lower usage fee. You book on the Internet, and your car will be waiting for you at your choice of forty-five high-demand locations across the city. Most of the cars are smallish — the Toyota Corolla is a standard — but if you need a van to pick up a bed, that can be arranged. If you want to show up at your class reunion in a Lexus, however, you'll have to work that out with a conventional car rental agency. Likewise for longer term rentals. AutoShare's major competitor, Zipcar (www.zipcar.com) operates on a similar basis.

AutoShare claims that its members save an average of $4,700 a year over the cost of private car ownership. Side benefits include significant advantages to the environment.

Walking or biking

Need we elaborate? It's not always possible, of course, but it's possible more often than we think. Free transportation and free fitness training rolled into one — that's a hard combination to beat!

Food

If you're like most of us, you used to cook. Home cookin' was the way we were brought up — that's the way good wives and good mothers fed their families. But then we got busy — very, very busy. And the prepared food business changed and expanded to meet our needs. Those terrible "TV dinners" that we used to hate morphed into the gourmet delights available in supermarkets now. And takeout too became ubiquitous, delicious...and expensive! We live in an era of convenience food — if it isn't delivered piping hot to our door, we're out eating at a restaurant. All of this costs money, lots of it. For most of us, food is one of our top three budget items. So if you're serious about reducing your living costs, you need to look hard at ways to reduce the cost of your daily bread.

Here are some basic rules. If you follow them, you can reduce the cost of eating without sacrificing anything in quality, taste, or nutritional value — we guarantee it! In fact, you'll almost certainly make improvements in your diet in all three of those areas.

Cook more

Once we're retired, we're not so busy. Our excuse for not cooking has disappeared, or at least receded. You've probably still got the cookbooks. If not, there are recipes galore in the newspapers and on the Internet. You've probably still got the know-how as well; you just need a little practice. And there are definite health benefits. You buy the ingredients, so you know what you're eating. Not only that, cooking can be fun. Preparing a meal with a spouse or other family members can be a regular, enjoyable social time.

Plan your menus

One food cost that is totally unnecessary is waste! In one of our crispers — to protect the guilty, we won't say which one — sits an organic broccoli and four peppers in four different colors. They looked wonderful in the grocery store, and they're packed with nutrition. But they're all destined for the compost because they didn't get used while they were fresh. Ten dollars' worth of vegetables down the drain! Multiply that $10 by fifty-two weeks in the year, and you've got a major leak in the food budget.

You can avoid this waste; it just takes planning. Make sure that the meat and the vegetables for the stir-fry are both in the refrigerator on the same day, and that you'll be home to cook and eat the stir-fry while those ingredients are still fresh. When you're working full time, you sometimes have to write off your good intentions. When you're retired, your standards can and should be higher.

Shop with a list

Supermarkets spend large amounts of money designing the layout of their stores so that you, the consumer, will drop even larger amounts of money on impulse purchases. Attractive, colorful displays are set up at the end of aisles. Non-food items that just might catch your eye are presented beside the checkout. The retailer will do whatever it takes to make you grab it and put it in your basket, whether you need it or not.

As a canny consumer, you're in a battle of wits with the merchants, who want you to buy, buy, buy! Your objective is to get in and out of the store with exactly what you need and not one item more. In this battle of wits, a list is an essential weapon. It will discipline your impulses, and cut down on both expense and waste.

Clip the coupons and shop the sales

Every week we are inundated with flyers from the grocery chains and other stores advertising price cuts and specials. If you need the product, these specials are often real deals, and you should follow up on them.

Beware, though! In the "shopping the sales" game you are again matching wits with brilliant professional merchandisers. Sale items are often "loss leaders," designed to get you into the store. Once you're there the merchants will go all out to seduce you into buying the higher-priced products as well. Really savvy shoppers never do. They plan their weekly menus around the specials in a number of different stores, and they go from store to store, buying only what's on sale. If you've got the time, and if you don't have to go out of your way and pay increased transportation costs to do it, it's certainly worth the effort. But if you decide your best bet is to do all your weekly shopping in the store that has the best bargains that week, stick to your list once you're there. You'll come out ahead.

Many advertisements contain "cents off" coupons, and in these days of high prices, "cents off" can quickly add up to dollars. Don't ignore these, but use them carefully. It goes without saying that you should never get fooled into buying a product you don't really need just because you happen to have a coupon. And have you ever noticed that coupons are almost always for brand-name products? Before you buy the sale item, check the house brand. You may get a much better deal, even without a coupon.

Buy house brands

Which brings us to house brands. We've already mentioned that house brands are typically clones of brand-name products. They're usually made in the same factories, using the same ingredients and the same processes. They're not cheaper because of their quality — they're cheaper because they're not as heavily advertised. Try them! They sometimes disappoint, but more often they're indistinguishable from their pricier sisters in fancier packages. You'll save a bundle.

Eat seasonal

We all know that the strawberries in January taste like wallpaper paste. They also cost twice as much as succulent local strawberries in June. So why do we buy them? We'd be better off — our budgets, our taste buds, and our overall health — buying our native fruits and vegetables when they're in season and exercising self-discipline when they're not. And if taste and cost alone don't convince you to resist those large red beauties, think about the environment. Those cardboard strawberries travel from California to Canada in the middle of winter in refrigerated trucks that belch out carbon dioxide emissions. If we all buy local apples instead, we'll be helping the environment.

Buy in bulk — sometimes

Buying in small quantities is almost always more expensive per unit than buying in bulk. As a general rule, buying case lots at the bulk outlets will save you money. If you've got cash flow problems, of course, you may not have the money to invest in cases of toilet paper or spaghetti sauce. And sometimes, if you shop the sales, you can do better than the bulk prices. In addition, it should go without saying that buying perishables in large quantities is no economy if you can't use them up before their "best before" dates. Frozen foods in bulk can be very good value, however, especially in winter when produce prices are sky-high.

So consider bulk purchasing, but be careful. Sometimes the bulk buy can be a false economy.

When you eat out, eat ethnic

Canada is a multicultural culinary paradise. If you live in any of our major cities, you can probably find restaurants serving the cuisine of at least twenty-five nations within a short walk from your home. And most of the people in those nations could feed their families for a *year* on what we're used to spending for our weekly groceries. Their national cuisines are interesting, varied, and tasty. They are also based on inexpensive foods, a fact that is reflected in the prices charged at their restaurants. Within two blocks of one major intersection in Toronto, it is possible to find a three-course lunch with tea at four restaurants of varying ethnicities for less than five dollars. Don't believe it? Get out there and look around.

Clothing

We've talked about the money you'll save on clothing simply because you won't be going to work every day. You won't need the power suits and the Ferragamo shoes. You won't need a new pair of pantyhose every day. You won't need to pay for weekly dry cleaning. Of course, you'll still want to dress in clothes that make you feel good. You still want to be warm, clean, and comfortable. You can't eliminate the expense entirely. So, what can you do to keep these costs to a minimum?

Look hard at your needs

What you need will depend on what you plan to do. Whatever that is, you will want to dress appropriately. You will also want to look good — whatever that means to you. But chances are that your retirement lifestyle will not require the latest in fashion. And you may not need quite so full a closet either. Remember that you've got more time now. You can do the laundry more often. If your best blouse is wrinkled, you'll have time to iron it. If your number one coat acquires a grease spot, you can use that handy little miracle stain remover you bought at Canadian Tire, and de-spot it yourself instead of sending it to the cleaners. You can try out those home dry cleaning products you throw in the dryer. You won't really need a "back-up" wardrobe any more.

Shop the sales

Clothing, like groceries, goes on sale all the time. The best bargains in big ticket items, like winter coats and boots, are often to be found on sale just before the season starts — the merchandise is in the stores, but you're not quite ready to think about winter yet, so the shopkeepers prime the pump with sale prices. With a little bit of planning, you can save big bucks. If you miss the pre-season sale, try to wait for the end-of season mark-downs. The selection isn't nearly as good, but the prices are even better.

Outlet stores

Outlet stores are everywhere these days. And fortunately for canny shoppers, they tend to cluster together in outlet malls, reducing the time and money needed to hunt them down. Outlet stores may be single-brand shops or "off-price" chains that bring together a wide variety of merchandise from cosmetics to clothing and luggage in a single location.

You should exercise some caution here. Outlet stores are usually selling the leftovers, last season's or last year's style — first quality merchandise that's just a bit dated. But some of these stores sell seconds and returns as well, so you'll have to be your own quality control inspector. Be careful; not everything in an outlet store is a bargain. It's helpful, before you buy, to have at least some sense of what comparable items would cost in a regular store. And as always, *don't buy anything you don't need, just because it's a bargain.*

If you live in southern Ontario, pick up a book called the *Shoestring Shopping Guide.* It comes out in a new and updated edition every year, and it's packed with listings for budget shoppers in a wide variety of categories. It also lists the main discount shopping malls in the region, and the current warehouse sales. If you can't get your hands on the book, you can also get Shoestring Shopping listings and information from their website: www.shoestringshopping.com. Registration is — of course — free. You should also check out www.pricenetwork.ca, which list deals, discounts, coupons, freebies, and warehouse outlets and sales all across the country.

Vintage clothing

"Vintage" clothing is often just a euphemism for clothing that somebody else owned before you did. It comes in a variety of styles, qualities, and "price points" (as the sales folk now say). At the low end, there's the Salvation Army and Goodwill, where we shopped when we were students. They're still around, and they haven't changed much. In the middle are businesses like Value Village. Some of our best friends clothe their entire families there. And at the high end, there are consignment stores that sell designer dresses, shoes, and handbags worn once or twice by the very rich, and then discarded as passé.

On the funky fringe, you can buy "real vintage" — Victorian night dresses, suits with padded shoulders from the forties and fifties, those lurid floral bell-bottoms we wore when we were in university, but these items often aren't cheap.

In all these places, luck plays a big role in how well you do on any given day. They don't always have exactly what you need, in the size and color you need, when you need it. But if you think of it as a treasure hunt it can be fun. Make it a habit to drop by and see the new arrivals.

Clothing exchanges

A money-saver that has recently been attracting attention is the clothing exchange. There's nothing formal about these exchanges — you can do it any way you want to. One popular model is the group of friends who get together for an evening, and bring with them all of their wardrobe mistakes — the lovely designer suit in exactly the wrong color, the silk trousers that were always a little too tight, the white linen suit that's always wrinkled or at the cleaners, the skirt that's too short or too long for your body type. The clothes are thrown into a pile in the middle of the room and *voila!*…one woman's fashion error is another woman's fabulous find.

Furniture

Used furniture, like used clothing, can be found in a wide variety of places at a wide variety of prices. All cities have their junk shops, and if you've got the time and the energy, you can find anything you want there. Country auctions can be worth a visit if you do your homework ahead of time about what's available. And if your tastes have become more refined since your student days, don't overlook the auction houses and consignment shops. The people who run these places are quite savvy, and unless you're really lucky, you won't find items underpriced. But you will often find very high quality furniture for a great deal less than you would pay for it new.

Travel

Many of us fantasize about retirement as a chance to travel and see the world. We'll finally have the time. But will we have the money? Fortunately, a little creativity can take us a long way.

Discounts

The major airlines have by and large stayed off the senior's discount bandwagon. But they've got something even more useful — heavily discounted fares for people who can travel at off-peak seasons and can commit to their travel dates and times. If you're used to traveling on business on someone else's nickel, you may not be aware of the dramatic differences in fare levels available to the leisure traveler. Here's a snapshot of the menu available from Air Canada. Don't make your travel plans on the basis of this chart. These prices are exclusive of taxes, and they change constantly. But you get the point. You'll find a comparable range of prices elsewhere.

Destination From Toronto	Best Discount Fare	Unrestricted Fare
Vancouver	$318	$918
Paris	$648	$2,720
Mexico City	$448	$2,480
Sydney, Australia	$1,562	$4,358
New York City	$278	$638

If you're prepared to accept that come hell or high water, you'll have to be on that plane at 6 p.m. on that particular Tuesday, you can fly for a fraction of what it would cost to buy an unrestricted ticket that allows you to fly whenever you want to and change your itinerary.

You can often do even better than these discount rates on smaller airlines, especially those catering to ordinary folk rather than business travelers. If you're traveling within Europe, there are amazing bargains to be had from companies like Ryanair if you don't have to make connections and don't mind arriving at out-of-the way airports in the middle of the night. But be careful — prices quoted usually don't include taxes (which can add up), the airlines don't feed you (at least not for free), and you may get hit with a significant extra charge because your modest luggage turns out to be "overweight" by the discounters' standards.

Check out these websites for finding and comparing discount airfares:

- **Canadian Affair**
  www.canadian-affair.ca
  This company offers flights on charter airlines like Thomas Cook, Air Transat and MyTravel, between various airports in Canada and various airports in the UK, at very low prices. The best deals are available for travelers who are prepared to risk booking "no change, no refund" tickets.

Rumor has it that Air Canada offers a seniors' discount of 10 percent. The rumor is true. The problem is that there's no discount on North American travel. Nor is there any discount on any international fare a budget-minded traveler would be likely to book. According to the Air Canada Reservations Line, the discount is available to those sixty-five and older flying executive class or higher to international destinations — as long as you didn't buy your ticket in a seat sale. If that's you, go for it!

- **Zoom Airlines**
  www.flyzoom.com

  Zoom Airlines offers flights to a number of airports in the UK from eight Canadian cities: Vancouver, Edmonton, Calgary, Winnipeg, Toronto, Ottawa, Montreal, and Halifax. You can also fly Zoom from Toronto, Montreal, Calgary, and Vancouver to Paris, France. Prices are attractive compared to traditional airlines: you can often get a seat on Zoom with a seat pitch that's almost Executive Class standard for the same price as Air Canada economy. There is a narrower choice of flight times, which can sometimes make connections a problem.

Trains do offer seniors' discounts. Likewise hotels and package tours may base some of their rates on age. But you're most likely to find bargains in these areas as well if you can be very flexible about when you travel, and can commit early to booking your trips.

House-swapping

If you're thinking of going away for a long vacation, consider the fact that you'll be leaving your current living accommodation vacant while you're away — a waste of money, and potentially hazardous if there are burglars in the neighborhood or severe winter temperatures that might freeze the pipes. Maybe you can find a tenant, but unless you're going to be away for a really significant period of time, that's not likely. Maybe you know an indigent student or an unemployed friend who will be happy to exchange their modest digs for your comfortable home for a few weeks to house-sit for you, but that's a long shot.

House-swapping can kill two birds with one stone. Let's say you live in British Columbia and you want to spend April in Arizona. The odds are that somebody in Scottsdale wants to spend a month in Vancouver — the weather's lovely in April, and the mountains are spectacular. The trick is to match you up with your counterparts, and arrange the swap.

There are companies that do just that — lots of them. To find them, search "house swapping" on the Internet. Each company works a little differently. On some sites, you pay an up-front listing fee; on others you don't pay until a suitable deal is actually struck. Some sites protect your privacy, brokering contacts for you with interested swappers. On other sites, you list your contact information, and people can then contact you directly. Sometimes cars are included in the exchange, which would reduce the cost of a holiday even further. Fees are quite nominal, compared to the cost of a conventional vacation. Some sites are free.

Some exchanges, such as www.intervac.com, are open to all comers. Others operate as specialty networks: www.seniorshomeexchange.com caters to seniors, while www.teacherstravelweb.com targets teachers.

Travel Insurance

Many younger travelers ignore travel medical insurance altogether, but seniors cannot afford to ignore this. In most cases, your provincial health plan will continue to cover you while you're abroad. (If you're going to be away for a longer period, check to make sure you will still have coverage.) If you require treatment while you're traveling, your provincial plan will reimburse you for part of the cost. Provincial repayment formulas differ; some provinces have a fixed ceiling, some will pay up to the Canadian cost for the services covered by Canadian public health insurance, and some will pay more than that. But none of them will simply pay the bill for foreign medical treatment, no questions asked. And health care costs aren't the same everywhere in the world. If you're traveling to countries with lower health care costs than those in Canada, you may be safe to leave home without supplementary insurance, as long as you're prepared to cover the cost of any services up front, wait to be reimbursed until you come back, and accept treatment at the normal standard of care for that country. If you're visiting a country where health care is more expensive, it can be a catastrophic error not to buy supplementary insurance before you go. Unfortunately, the United States, the favored destination for older Canadian tourists, is just such a country. Don't go to the U.S. without adequate supplementary health insurance unless you want to risk joining the burgeoning number of retirees who have had their retirement savings completely wiped out courtesy of the U.S. health care system.

If you've already got travel medical coverage through a retiree benefit plan or gold credit card, you can save the $125 a year and upwards a separate policy will cost you. Make sure you thoroughly understand what these policies cover and how they work. Some plans provide coverage for a limited number of days. If you are going to be away for longer than that, you should investigate whether you can purchase an extension, or buy "top-up" insurance to ensure you are covered for the full trip. The Canadian Snowbirds Association warns that some plans do not allow top-ups. Furthermore, some plans will refuse to pay at all if your trip is longer than the policy will cover you for. An additional pitfall is that many plans will not cover treatment for pre-existing conditions, so you'll be on your own if your arthritis flares up, or your high blood pressure leads to complications.

THE NICKELS AND DIMES

So much for the big ticket items. Let's move on now to the small stuff. It's not as painful as it sounds, and those nickels and dimes really do add up (remember the Latte Factor). Here are some suggestions.

Reschedule your luxuries

If you don't have to go to work, you can do your fine dining at lunchtime instead of at dinner time, for half the price. You can often go to concerts or the theater at lower prices too — by being spontaneous and buying same-day tickets. If you live in Toronto and don't know about T.O. Tix, check out the website at www.totix.ca. This service supplies same-day discount theater tickets for many productions. Same-day discounts can also be booked online, but you'll do better if you go right to the booth at Yonge and Dundas. Many Canadian cities offer the same central service. You can also call the box office directly for the show you're interested in, and check out whether discounts are available for last-minute seats.

Cheap movies

Cheap nights at mainstream commercial movie theaters are getting harder and harder to find. But in most Canadian cities, there is still have a thriving independent repertory cinema industry. The challenge is to find out where these are, and what's playing. A good source of information is your local college/university newspaper, which can usually be picked up for free around campus. Nobody's going to care that you're not a student. These publications list alternative commercial cinemas as well as cinema clubs, film festivals, and National Film Board offerings. You get much more value for your money at these theaters; even the regular prices are lower, often much lower, than the mainstream commercial theaters, and they usually have cut rates for seniors.

Free entertainment

Any city offers an abundance of free entertainment, if you know where to find it. Look for listings in the same resources you use for cheap movies: student newspapers or tabloids. Most towns and cities have websites listing festivals and upcoming events.

Loyalty programs

Many companies now offer perks to customers — usually in the form of points that can be accumulated and used for discounts on the purchase of additional merchandise. The object of these programs is to encourage customers to make that store their store of choice. So use these programs, by all means, but don't let them use you. The points are great, but they don't compensate for failing to comparison-shop.

The programs we like best are the ones where your points can be converted into cold hard cash instead of merchandise, even if that cash has to be spent in a particular store. With these programs, you can use points to buy items you really need *when they're on sale*. How thrifty is that!

Freecycling

Freecycling is a truly brilliant idea — it's an organization that matches people who have junk to give away with people prepared to give that junk a good home. It's web-based, naturally. Check out their website at www.freecyle.org and join a network in your area. There are many active local groups in all Canadian provinces and territories. You can unload the contents of your basement with a good conscience, and you can meet your own needs at the same time — for free!

Credit card deals

When it comes to credit cards, Canadians have a truly formidable array of choices available to them. Some offer low interest rates. Some offer points, or discounts on automobiles, or cash rebates. Some make contributions to charities on your behalf. The one that's the best deal for you will depend very much on your individual circumstances. For example, there are many types of cards that cater to travelers. If you travel a lot on Air Canada, there are several cards that allow you to accumulate points in Aeroplan. The TD Travel Gold Card and the Air Miles Card are more flexible; you have a choice of airlines. But you still have to book your travel through a particular travel agency. This may mean that you won't get the best price for your airline ticket. If you're really a bargain hunter and like to book your flights on the Internet, a card that offers a cash rebate will put money in your pocket for you to spend as you see fit.

The Financial Consumer Agency of Canada, a federal government service, offers a useful online tool for comparing different credit card packages. Go to www.fcac-acfc.gc.ca and check out their interactive credit card tool. The same website also offers an online tool for comparing bank service packages, another source of potential savings.

The ubiquitous seniors' discount

If you're a senior, you have many opportunities to get the same level of goods and services you did before you were retired, but pay a lot less for them. You've been waiting all your life for this one — use it!

In the world of the seniors' discounts, the term *senior* means different things to different people. To qualify for the Canadian government's seniors' identification card, you have to be sixty-five. But there are lots of companies that advertise seniors' discounts starting at age sixty. Some are available at fifty-five, or even fifty. So be sure to ask.

These discounts are so numerous and so varied that we can't list them all here. So we're going to send you to the Internet again. Check out www.wiredseniors.com. This is not a Canadian website, but it allows you to search only in Canada. Another helpful site is Canadian: www.senioryears.com, where you'll find lots of useful information and links, and also special sections on discounts. And check out the website run by the Canadian Association of Retired People (CARP): www.50plus.com. CARP members are eligible for many valuable discounts on hotels, insurance, travel packages, financial planning services, car rentals, and computers, among many other goods and services. CARP membership costs $19.95 a year for single or family membership.

And don't forget, some companies will provide an instant seniors' discount, even if they don't have a policy, if you just ask. Don't be shy! It's worth it.

CHAPTER 7

Housing

HOUSING IS A RETIREMENT PLANNING ISSUE

Retirement normally expands our housing horizons in many ways. You'll now have much more freedom and flexibility about where you live. Of course, there's no rule that retirees have to make changes in their housing. Many people love where they live and want nothing more than to stay put. If that's what you want to do, and you can afford it, than by all means choose that option. But the important thing to remember is that staying put is now just one option among many.

Let's look, for example, at geographic location. You are no longer fettered by your job to a particular city, or even a particular country. Some of the factors that went into your choice of a particular house within a community — proximity to work, ease and cost of commuting — all had to do with your work, and have disappeared. If you've lived in cities all your life, you might want to try rural or small town living. Maybe you live in Montreal and are tempted by the thought of milder winters on Vancouver Island. Maybe you've always hated leaving the cottage at the end of the summer, and dream of living there year-round. Retirement gives you those options. Now's your chance.

Retirement also brings more choices about what *type* of accommodation you live in. You probably don't need as much space as you once did. Your children have probably grown up and moved out. You don't need a home office. You won't need to do business entertaining. Smaller accommodation may suit you just fine. And even if you like lots of space around you, you may simply want to shed the burdens that come with maintaining that big house. If you don't like gardening, if you aren't "handy," if the constant appearance of dandelions in the lawn, damp spots on the basement walls, and cracks in the driveway asphalt are more of an irritant than a challenge, then maybe your dream retirement home is a townhouse or condo, where you can "contract out" the maintenance in exchange for a monthly fee. Perhaps you're retiring because you've got health problems. You may foresee the need for special adaptations in your accommodation and some assistance with the activities of daily living.

And of course there is the all-important question of expense. Maybe you think you've got the cost of housing covered. You bought your house many years ago and it's all paid for now. You've held your mortgage-burning ceremony, and your housing is now free, right? Wrong! Even if you're paying neither rent nor mortgage payments, your accommodation costs are still significant. If you live in a major city, your property taxes are high — maybe as much or even more than the mortgage payments you made when you first bought your house. Utility costs are sky-high and rising. All houses need constant maintenance. Older houses need constant repairs. Maybe you pay for cleaning or gardening or snow removal.

It all costs money. Housing eats up a very significant percentage of a household budget, even after the mortgage is paid off. On a retirement income, you may have a pressing need to find ways of cutting your accommodation costs. Or you may simply *want* to cut your accommodation costs to free up money for other choices — travel, a second home in an exotic location, setting up in a new part-time occupation, or maybe helping out with a down payment for an adult child starting a family.

STAYING PUT — ISSUES TO CONSIDER

You've cut your ties with the workplace, and that was a breeze! But the separation anxiety that accompanies parting with the family home may be harder. It's never a painless decision. There are all sorts of emotional attachments. You love your neighborhood. You've got friends and neighbors you're close to. You have a relationship with the dry cleaner and the butcher. You have wonderful local restaurants. You've sunk money into landscaping, and want to enjoy it. You've paid for a life membership at the nearby health club. You like the extra space — for the first time in your life, you've got a guest room! Your children or your parents live just round the corner or down the street. These are all good reasons to stay.

And a home is one of the few truly effective tax shelters in Canada. There's no capital gains tax on principal residences, so if your family home is increasing in value, that increase is tax free. If you decide to sell up and buy a cheaper residence or rent instead, and invest the profit you pocketed on the sale, you lose that protection. You'll pay tax on any investment income or capital gains.

So take your time and think about your decision. If you're a brand new retiree, you're still exploring what your new life is going to look like. If you don't want to leave, then stay put! But be sure that you're choosing to stay put for the right reasons. Here are some "don'ts" to think about:

- Don't live in the past. If it's both practical and logical to leave, and the only thing that's keeping you in place is your emotional ties to the family home, get over it!

- Don't let your children make the decision for you, especially if they don't live with you any more. Sentiment is cheap if you don't have to shovel the snow. They have their own lives, and they'll get over your "betrayal" very quickly.

- Don't let inertia clip your wings.

Your retirement dreams may be easier to realize if you give serious consideration to some of the accommodation options we discuss in this chapter.

Cutting Costs in Your Current Home

Maybe you're quite sure you don't want to move, at least not for a while. You've looked forward to retirement as a time when you can convert the spare bedroom to a sewing room, or set up a workshop in the basement or the garage. You've finally got a chance to do some serious gardening. If expense is an issue, are there ways to cut costs and stay put?

For some of you, the answer may be no. If you're already a very frugal steward of your domestic economy, then maybe there's no more fat to trim. But if you're like most of us, you've suffered perpetually from work-life imbalance. On the home front, your policy was "if it isn't an emergency I'll deal with it later," and then it got left for months or even years. The finer details of household management have been given short shrift. When you get a chance to focus, you may be shocked at how much money you've been squandering on low-value goods and services, simply because you've lacked the time to be more vigilant. But on the plus side, you'll be pleasantly surprised at how easily some of those high household bills can be substantially reduced. Here are some places to start:

- Check your telephone, Internet, and cable TV bills. Are you using all the service you pay for? You'd be surprised how many people are paying high prices for service packages they didn't even know they had. If you're spreading your business among a number of service

Environment Canada has a website providing access to information on all the energy conservation-related rebates available in Canada. You can search by province alone, or by province and type of program. Go to www.incentivesandrebates.ca.

providers, did you know that the major cable and telephone companies offer discounts for "bundling" phone, cable, and Internet services? Some of them also offer significant savings on long distance rates to customers who use their other services. You can save hundreds of dollars a year for the same level of phone, cable, and Internet service, just by checking out the deals and consolidating your business with one company.

- Review your home insurance coverage. Make sure you're not paying for riders on items that were lost or broken or discarded years ago. The policies are itemized, but how many of us actually read them at renewal time?

- You can save a lot on your electricity bills by cutting down on waste — turning lights off when you're not in the room, making sure the hot water taps don't drip, insulating pipes, putting the outdoor lights on a timer or a motion sensor, shutting windows in winter when the furnace is on, closing them in summer when the air conditioner is on, and weather-stripping the door and window sills. If you've got an old beer fridge in the basement, get rid of it. It's not energy efficient, and it's costing you a bundle just to keep it running. In British Columbia, B.C. Hydro has an old refrigerator disposal program; they'll come and pick it up, and will pay you $30 for it into the bargain.

- Do you have a programmable thermostat? The government tells us that installing a programmable thermostat will pay for itself in a year, and then save you 4.5 percent or more in annual energy costs. In many provinces, you'll get a rebate on your heating bill to sweeten the pot, just for buying the thermostat. If you have electric heating, consider electronic thermostats for your baseboard heaters. Some provinces pay rebates on these as well.

- How about those compact fluorescent light bulbs? A four-pack can save you almost $60 a year in energy costs. And most of you will use more than four. They're more expensive to buy than regular incandescent bulbs, of course, but it's well worth it. Rebate coupons for purchases of these bulbs are often available from local power companies.

- And when was the last time you really cleaned out your dryer vents — not just the vent *inside* your dryer, but also the exhaust vent to the outdoors? You'll be shocked at what's in there, and you'll love the money you save on your electric bill once you clear them out — probably at least $50 a year.

These are pretty painless economies, but they may make the difference between being able to stay in your own home and having to move to cheaper accommodation. But maybe you still can't cover all of your regular bills. Do you have to move? Not necessarily.

Generating Income from Your Current Home
How about a tenant?

If you've chosen to remain in your family home after the fledglings have flown, chances are good that you've got some extra space you don't need. Maybe it's just a room. Maybe it's the basement and it could be readily converted into a separate apartment. In either case, it's potential cash, if you need it.

Renting out single rooms is relatively hassle-free. In most municipalities, there are no zoning issues you need to be concerned about. A separate apartment may be a different proposition. Your neighborhood may be zoned for single-family dwellings, and you may need to get special permission before you can convert your home to multiple units. Most larger municipalities encourage basement conversions. It creates inexpensive housing in a tight market. So there may be some time-consuming paperwork to go through, but you can probably get permission in the end if you want to do it.

In order to get some idea of how much supplementary income you could realistically generate from your home, check your local papers to find out what rents are being asked in your area. Attractive one-bedroom basement apartments in east-end Toronto can rent for close to $10,000 a year. That's taxable income, of course, so you'll have to declare it on your tax return. And it won't be clear profit. You'll have some expenses as well — the conversion costs, of course, as well as on-going expenses for items like advertising, cleaning, and maintenance. But in return, you can take corresponding deductions for the costs involved in earning the income, including a portion of your household operating expenses.

Reverse mortgages

Another method for extracting money from a paid-up house is a reverse mortgage. This is a financial product available to Canadians who are sixty and older. Although a reverse mortgage can be arranged at any Canadian financial institution, all such mortgages in Canada have the same ultimate source: a private company called the Canadian Home Income Plan (see their website, www.chip.ca, for further information).

Reverse mortgages work like this. Think back to when you first bought your house. You made a down payment, usually 25 percent of the value of the house. You borrowed the rest of the purchase price in a lump sum from the bank. You then gave that lump sum to the vendor. Once you did that, the house belonged to you. But in effect you only owned 25 percent of the equity (or value); you owed the other 75 percent to the bank.

You had to repay the loan of course, over a number of years in monthly payments. To secure the loan, the bank held a mortgage on your house. If you didn't make your monthly payments, the bank could seize your house and sell it to repay the loan. As you paid off portions of the mortgage principal, your share of the equity increased. Once your payments were all made, you owned your house free and clear. In other words, you owned 100 percent of the equity in your house.

With a reverse mortgage, you're extracting that equity to use for other purposes. The mechanics are basically the same as a conventional mortgage. You borrow money from the bank, and as security for that loan, the bank puts a mortgage on your house. The amount you can borrow depends on a number of factors, including your age, the age of your spouse, and the value of your home. Currently the amount of any reverse mortgage is capped at $500,000, even if the value of your home is considerably higher.

There are two important differences between reverse mortgages and conventional mortgages. The first is that you don't have to turn over the money you borrow to any vendor, since you already own the house. You keep it for yourself. You may take it out as a lump sum, or it may be paid out in staggered or periodic payments. The choice is yours. (That's the "reverse" part — the bank pays you instead of you paying the bank.) The money you get is tax free, since it represents the equity in your principal residence, so it doesn't trigger any claw-back of OAS or GIS. The second difference — and this is really the attractive feature for most retirees considering a reverse mortgage — is that you don't have to pay back the money as long as you own the house. The bank is prepared to be patient and wait for its money out of the proceeds of sale. The timing of the sale is in your hands. If you (and your spouse, if you have one) stay in the house as long as you live, you never have to pay it back. It's a problem for your estate.

But here's the catch. Like any loan, your reverse mortgage loan is accumulating interest. In the case of a reverse mortgage, that interest rate is higher than the rate on a conventional mortgage. Because you're not making any payments on the loan, the accumulated interest is being added to the principal amount you borrowed. When it comes time to sell the house, you'll owe the bank a whole lot more than you borrowed. The bank takes the risk that you'll outlive the value of your house — if you live long enough, the amount secured by the mortgage can increase beyond the fair market value of the property. But banks are nothing if not good at making money, and they price reverse mortgages at a level designed to ensure that they almost always win the bet about how long you'll live. It's not uncommon for the bank to get almost the entire value of the house. There'll be little or nothing left for your estate.

That's fine if that's what you want. It was your money that paid for the house in the first place, and if living in it until the end of your days is your first priority, a reverse mortgage may be your cup of tea. But unless you care very much about remaining in a particular house, you (and your heirs) are probably better off if you sell a house you can no longer afford, invest the proceeds and use the investment income to meet the gap between revenues and expenses. Don't kid yourself that a reverse mortgage is a way to save the house for your estate. Unless you're hit by a bus the day after you sign the agreement, it's not likely going to work that way. Reverse mortgage financial products are marketed to retirees as a mechanism for staying in your family home when you can no longer really afford to. They do that, of course. But at a high price! So be very careful that you've explored the issue from all sides and identified the real costs and benefits before you agree to put a reverse mortgage on your house.

DOWNSIZING
Is It Time for a Condo?

For many people, the freedom to downsize is one of the first benefits of retirement. They seize their chance as soon as they can. You may be seriously considering doing the same — selling the family home and moving to accommodation that is more appropriate to your family's current size, lifestyle, and budget. Downsizing may involve moving to a community where housing is less expensive. It may involve moving from a detached four-bedroom house to a two-bedroom condo. Or maybe you fancy a townhouse beside a golf course in rural Saskatchewan, an oceanside salt box in Nova Scotia, or a double-wide in a desert town in Arizona.

Downsizing can be an exciting project. After all, the world is now your oyster — at least in theory. For the first time in your life you can move anywhere you like. But don't let your enthusiasm swamp your common sense. You should proceed along the downsizing path with extreme caution! Make sure you've got all the facts and thought through all of the pros and cons before you uproot. Mistakes can be traumatic. And costly.

The City Mouse and the Country Mouse

It goes without saying that some people love living in the city, and some people love living in the country. It's a rare person who likes both. So before you make an impulsive move from the city to the country, or to a small town, ask yourself:

- Do I like living in the city?

- If I like it, what do I like about it? Will I find those things in the country as well? If not, what will I substitute for the pleasures I get from city life?

- If I hate it, why? Will the country really suit me better?

Be very honest with yourself. Now is not the time to indulge romantic dreams of solitude if you know in your heart that you're naturally gregarious, and can't live without a convenience store five minutes away.

If you're moving to reduce your living expenses, be very sure that the move will give you the savings you need. Remember — a house that is cheaper to buy may not necessarily be cheaper to live in. You may plan to pocket the difference between the price of your old home and the price of the new home, and invest it to generate income. But if the operating costs for your new abode are significantly higher than those for the old, this may wipe out the cost advantage entirely. You wouldn't be the first retiree to find out that electric heat for the bungalow cottage in winter costs significantly more than the high efficiency gas furnace you recently installed in your tall, narrow semi-detached house in the city. And if your dream is a small country "estate," don't forget to factor in the cost of ploughing out that long tree-lined lane after every snowstorm, and keeping that broad swath of lawn trimmed and green throughout the summer. Unless you're planning on doing a lot of the labor yourself — and you won't be able to do that forever! —you may find that country life is not as economical as you thought.

MOVING TO A FOREIGN COUNTRY

Many prospective retirees dream of leaving Canada altogether. In some cases, they want to return to their roots — to the country they or their parents or grandparents left behind when they immigrated to Canada. In other cases, they are in quest of a milder climate. Regrettably, Canada offers retirees no choices like Arizona and Florida within our own borders. The best we can do is Victoria, where it still snows and the average temperature in January is still a chilly 6.5 degrees Celsius. While this compares favorably to Montreal or Iqaluit, it can't compete with Mexico for older bones.

We can all dream! But if you're serious about a move to Mexico, Costa Rica, or Spain, make sure you look before you leap. Seniors' magazines are full of stories about retirees who moved to foreign parts (or sometimes only as far as a chalet in the Laurentians, which can seem like a foreign country in winter) and lived to regret it. Here are just a few of the numerous issues that must be considered:

- Does the country you want to move to have restrictions on foreign ownership? Or an unfamiliar and unreliable system of land tenure that may leave you in the lurch at some point?

- If you cease to be a Canadian resident, what will happen to your health care and other social benefits? How will you replace them?

- Have you taken expert advice about your income tax situation if you become a resident of a foreign country? Remember, this can vary from country to country, depending on specific tax agreements between Canada and your new home country. So advice about a move to Spain may not hold for Belize or Costa Rica.

- How does the cost of living in the specific place you want to relocate compare to your current cost of living? Don't go by general figures for the country as a whole — if you're moving to a local hot spot for foreign residents, the costs will inevitably be considerably higher than average.

- What will you do about currency fluctuations? If your income is in Canadian dollars, it may not go as far as you think. Exchange rates can go up or down dramatically, and that can make a huge difference, since you'll be paying your bills in local currency.

We're not counseling overcaution. There's never reward without risk. But do make sure you've asked the right questions and got answers that take into account your specific situation. Mistakes in this area can be very costly in the long run. Avoid them if you can.

The Canadian government provides a website full of information for Canadians living or hoping to live abroad. Check out www.voyage. gc.ca, and download the pamphlet *Retirement Abroad: Seeing the Sunsets*. It will give you at least preliminary answers to some of your questions, and steer you towards other useful resources.

LIVING WITH YOUR CHILDREN

Back in the days of the Old Retirement, it was commonplace for retired parents, worn out from work and unable to continue to make a living, to find shelter in the homes of their adult children. It was expected. Your parents looked after you when you were too young to earn your keep, and you returned the favor in their old age. In most cases, multi-generational families simply did not have the resources to maintain multiple households. The grandparents lived with the extended family out of necessity. This necessity has now morphed into a cultural tradition in some communities.

But times have changed. You and your son or daughter may be very close, but think carefully before you agree to joint living arrangements. We'll discuss this in more detail later. Suffice it here to say that like all retirement options, it is a change that should be embarked upon only with caution, and only after carefully reviewing the pros and cons. It's not an easy transition for either side of the generation gap.

RETIREMENT HOUSING

In addition to conventional housing options, there is also "retirement housing." Because moving house has become a commonplace of retirement planning, whole industries have evolved to cater to the housing needs of retirees. There's something for everyone out there — recreational condominium communities built up around golf courses, co-op housing, retirement homes, supportive housing, combinations of retirement and nursing homes, and, of course, nursing homes. Both non-profit agencies and the private sector have developed a wide variety of imaginative housing initiatives designed to meet the needs of seniors in local communities. The terminology can be confusing, particularly since many of these housing categories overlap. The common denominator is that retirement housing tends to offer a blend of shelter and services, often including some health care services, to older Canadians who are not in the workforce.

Some of these arrangements are private sector, for-profit developments within which housing and other services are purchased at market rates. Some of them are creative private arrangements developed by groups of friends and colleagues. Some of them are run by non-profit organizations and charities, may target particular ethnic, religious groups or occupational groups, and may subsidize fees. Where health services are a significant part of the package, these facilities are typically government regulated, with government health insurance contributing all or a significant proportion of the costs of the care provided.

If you're interested in housing designed specifically for retirees, it's important to understand what the options are. Let's look at some of them in more detail.

Retirement Communities

You see advertisements for these developments in the newspapers every weekend — golf communities north of Toronto, skiing communities near Whistler, year-round recreational communities in Banff and the Laurentians. They are usually combinations of low-rise and townhouse residential units, offering condominium ownership and hefty monthly fees to pay for the landscaping and maintenance and shared recreational facilities.

These commercial developments target retirees, offering the specific types of recreational facilities and social amenities that will attract homogeneous groups with shared interests and lifestyles. In practical terms, however, they are indistinguishable from any other condominium development. Units are bought and sold like any other condominium. The human rights codes that apply to all housing in Canada apply to these developments, and they cannot legally discriminate against buyers on grounds of age or employment status. In practice, it does not make business sense to disqualify potential buyers on the grounds that they still have jobs. So these are retirement communities only because retirees choose to congregate there.

There is no special government regulation of these communities, and no government subsidies for the cost of living there.

Life Lease Facilities

Developments offering "life leases" to residents can now be found in many Canadian communities. These facilities offer a range of housing options, from shared accommodation to apartments and townhouses. Unlike the retirement communities discussed above, they do not sell living space outright. What they sell to their residents is a capital interest, which can be resold if the buyer leaves or dies. This interest is usually a leasehold, not a condominium interest, which means that it is a "right to occupy" the unit, sometimes for a limited period of time, rather than an ownership interest. Because a right to occupy has less value on the open market, a life lease is normally less costly than outright ownership. These facilities also charge monthly fees to cover the costs of maintenance and shared facilities and services.

Most life lease communities for retirees currently operating in Canada are developed, owned, and operated by non-profit organizations. They often cater to quite specific religious or ethnic communities. The costs are usually lower as a result. Entry to the facility may be restricted to members of the sponsoring organization, and leases can only be resold to persons who would qualify for admission into the facility. In principle, of course, there is no reason why the private sector could not provide retirement facilities in which residents bought life leases instead of ownership interests, as long as admission to the facility was open to all. This model, popular in the U.S., is not yet widespread in Canada, but it's on its way.

Retirement Homes

Retirement homes are also unregulated, and except in Alberta, which provides a limited subsidy for some seniors, residents pay their own costs. The accommodation provided ranges from shared rooms to multi-bedroom apartments. Costs vary — the Ontario Ministry of Health website estimates a range of $1,500 to $5,000 monthly for this type of retirement accommodation, although the sky's the limit, with more luxurious facilities opening all the time.

Retirement homes differ from retirement communities in a couple of important respects. First of all, they normally provide some level of assistance with the activities of daily living, such as housekeeping, meals, and personal care. Emergency assistance is usually available twenty-four hours a day, although these facilities do not provide nursing care. Secondly, retirement homes are legally permitted to restrict accommodation to those who need their services for purposes of independent living. This means that they are almost exclusively occupied by seniors, although they may also cater to younger residents with disabilities.

Retirement homes are also known as retirement residences, congregate housing, or assisted living facilities.

The *Care Guide* is a useful resource for information on housing options for retirees. The website, www.careguide.ca, is a gold mine of listings and resources. It also provides a free hard copy publication available in regional editions for British Columbia, Alberta, Eastern and Northern Ontario, and South Western Ontario; ordering information is on the website. If you don't need this resource for yourself yet, you might need it for your parents.

Supportive Housing

"Supportive housing" caters to seniors whose needs are similar to those of retirement-home residents. The difference is that these facilities are run by non-profit organizations or municipal governments. The term is often used in reference to social housing projects specifically targeted to seniors, in which rent subsidies and social services are available.

Long-Term Care Facilities

Long-term care (LTC) facilities, also known as nursing homes, are available only to people who need a high level of personal care, and whose medical condition justifies access to nursing care twenty-four hours a day. LTC facilities in all provinces in Canada are government regulated and because they offer significant social services including medical care, they are heavily subsidized as well. In Ontario, this subsidy is offered through a system of co-payments: in 2006–2007, individual residents paid $1,513.53 a month for standard accommodation, $1,756.87 for semi-private, and $2,061.04 for private accommodation, and the government covered the additional cost. People who require nursing home care and cannot afford the co-payment receive government assistance with the cost of basic accommodation.

In Ontario, agencies known as Community Care Access Centres (CCACs) currently act as gatekeepers to long-term care facilities. While a CCAC referral is necessary for admission, there is some degree of personal choice involved in the placement process. Prospective residents can identify three preferred placements; if they turn down a bed offered at any of these, they are removed from all waiting lists, but can apply again in six months. If they accept a second or third choice, they can remain on the waiting list for their first choice, and move when a spot becomes available. Those who are prepared to and able to wait will usually end up in the facility of their choice eventually.

Additional information about CCACs and the long-term care

system in Ontario can be found at www.health.gov.on.ca. Other provinces have a variety of placement systems; consult the ministry of health in your province for information.

Combination Facilities

While long-term care facilities are government regulated, they are frequently owned and operated by the same for-profit companies that own and operate retirement homes. These companies often run both types of facilities side by side, obtaining economies of scale from the co-management of common services like housekeeping and food preparation. They provide residents with a form of one-stop shopping. Residents may have to move into a different part of the facility when they require long-term care, but they do not have to disrupt their lives by moving to an entirely new environment at a time when they may be fragile and find it difficult to adapt. Such combination facilities also permit spouses to stay closer together, since the spouse in better health can stay in the retirement home even when the frailer spouse moves into long-term care.

CHAPTER 8

Why Work?

Work is one of the most fundamental aspects in a person's life, providing the individual with a means of financial support and, as importantly, a contributory role in society. A person's employment is an essential component of his or her sense of identity, self-worth and emotional well-being.

Mr. Justice La Forest, judge of the Supreme Court of Canada, in the *Reference re Public Service Employee Relations Act (Alberta)* [1987] 1 Supreme Court Reports 313

RECLAIMING WORK IN RETIREMENT

When we think of retirement, we usually think of leaving work behind us. Isn't "work in retirement" an oxymoron? We're retiring, after all. Why on earth are we talking about making a *work* plan?

To answer that question, we need to look more closely at the meaning of work. Work is one of the most utilitarian words in the English language, and one of the most flexible. The *Oxford English Dictionary* takes a full ten pages to cover its myriad uses. But for our purposes, the first OED definition says it all: work is "something that is or was done; what a person does or did; an act, deed, proceeding, business." In other words, work is what we *do*. In the modern world, however, that generous definition has been constricted almost beyond recognition. Work is never what we *want* to do. Work is always what we *have* to do. And even more narrowly, work is what we're *paid* to do. We work because we must, to earn a living. We work to pay the bills.

It wasn't always this way, of course. Over the course of human history, many societies valued creative and productive activity for its own sake. In ancient Greece, citizens never engaged in paid labor. Free men had more important responsibilities — the management of the state and the intellectual realm. In Victorian England, the ambitious industrialist aspired to amass a fortune as soon as possible so that he could join the leisured ranks of the country gentlemen. Once he had attained his goal, however, he threw himself into politics, philosophical inquiry, estate management, polar exploration, natural history, or any one of hundreds of other serious pursuits. As a gentleman *amateur*, he was productive and respected, making important contributions to arts and letters, to the advancement of science and human knowledge in general — for love, not money.

But by the end of the nineteenth century, the market had triumphed. From then on, only the professional historian, the professional classicist, the professional botanist was worthy of respect. The gentleman farmer was replaced by scientific farming and agribusiness. The realm of work, important work, valuable work, had now become co-extensive with the realm of paid work. And it is in this world that we, the generation now contemplating retirement, came to adulthood and lived our working lives. We equate work with the labor market. But it's simply not so.

Psychologists and philosophers, who understand these things much better than economist and financiers do, remind us that work is what we *do*; it is our productive and creative activity. They also tell us that our productive, creative activity fulfills many fundamental human needs. It is our work that gives us:

- a sense of personal competence
- a sense of self-worth
- intellectual stimulation
- scope for our creativity
- community, and a framework for growth in our social relationships
- continuing challenges — physical, mental and spiritual — that create opportunities for personal growth
- a satisfying structure for our days
- variety in our lives.

Those are important needs! Can we really contemplate leaving all of that behind us when we retire? Is it realistic or practical — above all, is it wise — to embark on retirement, another half a lifetime, without a plan for meeting those needs?

Of course not. We know we need work. Even if you're one of the lucky ones who can meet all of your material needs without paid work — and you know who you are by now — it's clear that you will still need work. But if we are going to find satisfaction in retirement work, we have to discard the notion that we are defined by what we earn. We have to rid ourselves of the idea that only paid work is real work. We need to reclaim the older, richer notion that work is what we do, not just what we're paid to do.

Some of us will be able to relate to the psychological importance of work more readily than others. For those of you whose careers really did meet all the needs the psychologists talk about, nurturing your spirit as well as your body, confirming your place in the universe, it will have real resonance. You will almost certainly have a special ambivalence about

Psychologists define human needs by reference to a paradigm called **Maslow's Hierarchy of Needs**, developed in the mid-twentieth century by Abraham Maslow and first published in an influential book called *Motivation and Personality*. Maslow argued that human beings are universally motivated by five groups of needs. Although some of these needs are "higher" than others (hence the term "hierarchy"), healthy growth and development throughout our lives requires that all these needs be met.

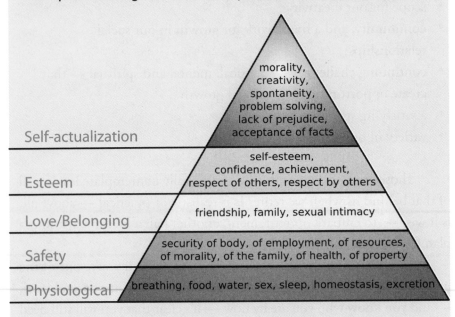

Self-actualization — morality, creativity, spontaneity, problem solving, lack of prejudice, acceptance of facts

Esteem — self-esteem, confidence, achievement, respect of others, respect by others

Love/Belonging — friendship, family, sexual intimacy

Safety — security of body, of employment, of resources, of morality, of the family, of health, of property

Physiological — breathing, food, water, sex, sleep, homeostasis, excretion

The money we earn from work helps us meet our lower order needs. It is work itself that addresses our higher needs.

leaving all that behind you. But you will also understand the soul-satisfying importance of good work, and you'll be motivated to fill the gap your career job has left behind. For many others, after thirty or forty years, your jobs simply don't meet these needs, at least not any more. For you, the good news is that the kind of work you need to grow and thrive as human beings is still out there. It can be found in the labor market if that's what you want and need. But it can be found just as easily outside the wage economy — maybe even more easily.

KNOW THYSELF

> "Most people want to work, by being creative, active, caring for those they love and helping others whether altruistically or in the expectation that they will be helped when they need help. The human being wants to build, to make and to understand. Above all, we use work to become, to extend ourselves. The motivation comes from our conscious and unconscious drives, from our culture and from our history."
>
> Guy Standing, *Beyond the New Paternalism: Basic Security as Equality*, Verso, 2002, pp. 242-243

So it's back to the job hunt.

Whether we're looking for paid work, volunteer activities, further education, travel, or simply those recreational activities we usually call play, we need to step carefully in our search for post-retirement work. We need to think long and hard about what kind of work will meet our needs. We need to take a thorough personal inventory: strengths and weaknesses, passions, unfulfilled ambitions, pleasures, needs, and wants. The success of our retirement will depend on the choices we make now.

Flash back to an earlier stage in your life, when you were deciding what to be when you grew up. You emerged from the cocoon of family and school, tested your strengths and discovered your weaknesses in the real world. You lived through much angst and uncertainty. But you experienced it all as exhilarating — a time in your life when the possibilities seemed unlimited, when all you saw was open water ahead!

You were in your twenties then. You're not, of course, in your twenties any more. And it's only realistic to acknowledge that not being twenty has its downside. You don't have quite as much energy. You're less inclined to take risks. You feel that there's not much time to learn new skills and acquire experience. And even if you're bored or burnt out in your job — and not all of us are, not by a long shot — you're used to a certain comfort level, a feeling of competence and confidence that comes from knowing that you've mastered what you do, and you do it well. The idea of change, of starting all over again, can be daunting.

But not being twenty also has enormous advantages. You've earned the confidence that comes from having one success under your belt already. You know yourself better. You've got more options, because you've got a financial cushion. You're not looking at decades of crushing expenses — the mortgage is paid off and the kids are old enough to fly on their own if need be. You don't have to be nearly so practical. There's no reason why the possibilities for work in retirement can't be as unlimited as they were back then, when you were choosing your first career. But you must choose what you do now with equal care if you want your retirement work to meet your needs.

There is plenty of help available. A whole career-assessment, coaching, and counseling industry is waiting to advise you. Most of it isn't tailored specifically for retirees. A retirement coaching industry is gathering momentum out there, but it's still pretty new, and while we're waiting, we'll have to adapt for our purposes the myriad resources directed at mid-life career changers — people who've been downsized, or people who are unhappy in their work and considering major shifts mid-career. If you're struggling with the issue of whether you should leave your career job behind, uncertain about what you would put in its place after retirement, you'll have a great deal to learn from these resources. Because the basic principle is the same: KNOW THYSELF!

Here are some suggestions for where to find guidance:

- **Books**

  Comb the self-help shelves of the bookstores and the libraries. They're loaded with books like *What Color Is Your Parachute?* Written by Richard Bolles, first published in 1970, and updated annually ever since, this guide has sold millions of copies. Can that many readers be wrong? One of the first of the employment self-help books, it's been dubbed "the job-hunter's bible." You might also want to look at a couple of books by Toronto-based Barbara Moses: *What Next?: The Complete Guide to Taking Control of Your Working Life*, or *Career Intelligence: 12 New Rules for Work Life and Success*. We've listed some other helpful resources in the Further Reading section for this chapter in the back of the book.

- **The Internet**

  The Net offers a wide variety of online psychometric tests that will help you gain insight into your personality type, together with ideas about what type of work you might find most satisfying. Some of these tests are free; others provide you with preliminary reports free, but charge fees for fuller reports. Before you spend time and money on Internet testing, however, check out www. jobhuntersbible.com, run by Richard Bolles the author of *What Color Is Your Parachute?* This very helpful website, which provides a wealth of information and links to other Internet resources on career counseling and job hunting, also provides a detailed critique of Internet testing services, and directs you to the websites, both free and fee-based, which the author finds most useful.

- **Career counseling services**

  Try the services at your local YWCA or YMCA. They don't come cheap, but they offer a professional, comprehensive service for less than you're likely to pay on the private market. If you really want to go for broke, of course, there are reputable full-service career coaches, counselors, and job search agencies. If you've been forced to retire from a job, your "golden handshake" may include the offer of outplacement services from one of these firms, including aptitude testing and assessment. By all means accept, even if you don't plan to put yourself on the job market again in the conventional sense. You're bound to get some useful insights that will help you figure out what kind of work you are most likely to succeed in and enjoy in retirement.

SEEKING A NEW BALANCE

Even for those of us still in full-time jobs, paid work is only part of the work we do on a daily basis. Retirement will not turn our to-do list into a blank page. As working women, we structured our lives to include both paid and domestic responsibilities. For most of us the unpaid commitments included child care, and although that is now less demanding (we hope!), we may now have taken on the care of other family members. What we will be seeking in retirement is a new version of the classic work-life balance, one that with some careful planning and a little luck will have plenty of space for *us*, for the things that give us pleasure and satisfaction, for the things we want to do.

Some of us have been fortunate enough to find room in our pre-retirement lives for travel or volunteer work, hobbies or a cultural life, and for such basic health maintenance activities as regular exercise. Many working women in Canada are involved in volunteer activities long before they retire. Many have active hobbies and challenging fitness routines. For these women, a retirement work plan may involve simply redeploying time that used to be allocated to paid work, and redirecting it to other activities they already know and love.

Others will find themselves suddenly free in a brand-new way. For those of us whose lives were full to the brim with work and home duties, the loss of our career employment will open a very large gap. We may greet the prospect of vast tracts of unscheduled time with delight or with foreboding. But if we are not used to allocating discretionary time, we may find the task of designing a work plan more of a challenge.

The building blocks for a post-retirement work plan are many and various. We can choose from a menu that includes:

- reduced working hours
- a new career
- self-employment
- working abroad
- volunteer activities
- further education
- recreational travel
- hobbies
- athletic activities.

And of course, our work plan needs to leave room for the work involved in keeping our finances in order, maintaining family and outside relationships, developing new friendships and community ties, and keeping ourselves as fit and healthy as we possibly can. It's a pretty full plate we're preparing. But remember, the odds are that we'll have lots of time to savor every morsel of it.

Regardless of what your needs are now, remember that your needs and resources may change over time. Right now you may want or need supplementary income to bridge an income gap until you start drawing CPP, OAS, pension, or RRIF income. But ten years from now you may want to leave paid work behind you. You need to think ahead about how you will fill your days when that time comes. You may be looking forward to a leisurely, unhurried retirement with your spouse, a perpetual holiday with no cares and no responsibilities, and right now you may have enough money to fund it. But a year or two down the road things could be different. You may find yourself bored to death, or widowed, or broke. While enjoying Plan A, you need to think about what will happen if you need or want to go to Plan B. Next, we'll consider a variety of options for work in retirement, both paid and unpaid.

CHAPTER 9

More
Sustainable Jobs

WORKING MORE SUSTAINABLY

If you've decided you'll be staying in the workforce for a while longer, you need to find a way to make that happen. For many of us, this will mean a serious renegotiation of our relationship with the workplace. It will involve working more sustainably. If we're going to work longer, most of us will want to work smarter.

> EKOS Research recently conducted a research study entitled "What are Canadians' Preferences with Regard to Retirement?" EKOS reported that "everyone loves to work, but no one likes their job." Canadians will work "past retirement" only if they are offered enjoyable work, and *less of it*.
>
> EKOS Research Associates, Inc., December 14, 2004

One of the major achievements of the trade union movement in the twentieth century was the passage of social legislation limiting the hours of work for industrial laborers, mandating paid vacations, and banning or limiting compulsory overtime. In the late nineteenth century, most industrial workers worked ten-hour days, six days a week. There were no vacations. By the middle of the twentieth century, the eight-hour day and the five-day week were the standard, with a paid vacation of two weeks in North America, and there was pressure to increase that to the European norm of six weeks a year. It looked like we were on our way to some real work-life balance. But a funny thing happened on the way to the end of the century. We got busier. Hours of work starting *increasing* again. We were back on the treadmill, running faster and faster. A culture of workaholism took hold. Note the coincidence here; the pace of work started to pick up again in earnest just when women began to enter the workforce in large numbers. It's no wonder we're feeling burned out. We *are* burned out!

Are we wearing out as well as burning out? Not really. We're older, there's been wear and tear on our bodies, and we don't always have the energy we had when we embarked on our careers. But unless we've done hard physical work all our lives, we're probably just as fit to perform our jobs as we ever were. If we're contemplating retirement, it's not because we're no longer up to the job, it's just that our priorities have shifted. We don't want to work ourselves into the grave, and we don't need to.

We've heard throughout our working lives about work-life balance. As women, we've been somewhat ambivalent about that concept. In many professions, women who sought work-life balance in the form of part-time work or flex-time were relegated to the "mommy track," as second-class employees. And however we felt about work-life balance, very few of us ever achieved it. Now, perhaps we can. We can afford to work fewer hours. And we're no longer so concerned about a negative impact on career advancement. We still want work, but we want less of it. We want our work to be more flexibly scheduled. And we want it to be interesting.

"There are two basic schools of thought about retirement behaviour. One school says people retire for economic reasons related to living standards. People prefer leisure to work, and retire when they feel they have enough money to support retirement...A second school of thought suggests that retirement is driven less by income per se, than by the quality of life before and after retirement, particularly related to job and workplace quality. People retire because leisure is preferable to the jobs they actually have, but if appropriate jobs were available, people would prefer to work than to retire. They would prefer a combination of higher overall standard of living and a more balanced distribution of leisure over the course of life (with greater work-life balance being, in turn, an integral part of job and workplace quality) than early retirement."

PRI Project, "Population Aging and Life-Course Flexibility: The Pivotal Role of Increased Choice in the Retirement Decision," March 2004

There are lots of options for "bridge employment," a term that's gaining currency to describe the jobs of people making a transition towards retirement. Let's look now at some bridge options.

POSTPONING RETIREMENT

One obvious way to increase the income you will have in retirement is to stay in your job longer. There's no doubt that early retirement has a compounding negative effect on retirement savings. The earlier you retire, the fewer years you have to save for retirement, and the longer you need to be able to live off your retirement savings. Postponing retirement turns that compounding effect into a positive. We have a longer period in which to save for retirement, and fewer years in which we have to live off those savings.

"Based on the 1998-99 National Population Health Survey...the average 63-year-old Canadian male can expect to be free of activity limitation to over 75 years of age, whereas the average female of the same age can expect to be free of activity limitation until the age of 78."

Sarah Hogan and Jeremey Lise, Health Canada, "Life Expectancy, Health Expectancy and the Life Cycle", *Policy Research Initiative,* Volume 6, Number 2, http://policyresearch.gc.ca

Postponing retirement can improve your projected retirement income dramatically. The math is very real. Try it out on an Internet retirement calculator. Run your calculations through on the assumption that you will retire at age fifty-five and will be retired for thirty years. Then try it again assuming you will retire at age sixty and be retired for twenty-five years. Advancing your expected date of retirement by five years reduces by a astonishing amount the total lump sum you will need to fund your retirement. It gets even better if you maintain a constant RRSP savings rate until you retire. And if you just keep on working forever, you won't need any retirement income at all! Just kidding, but you get the point.

A strategy for increasing retirement income that depends on staying longer in harness and having fewer years to enjoy the fruits of your labor may not be very attractive to most Canadians on the cusp of retirement. We've worked hard for decades and we want a change. But there may be ways you can modify the job to make it sustainable for longer. Change is always difficult and a more manageable version of what we've been doing all along has a lot of attractions. It's more appealing than wading back into the job market or joining the myriad ranks of the self-employed.

An obvious option is going part-time — keep your job, but simply do less of it. But is this really a practical option? Will employers, who resisted all our efforts to create women-friendly, family-friendly (or even human-being friendly!) workplaces for thirty years and more, suddenly turn around and allow their older employees to work part-time, flexible schedules? Some of them won't, of course. But we may be in for some surprises here, because at this point, demography is on our side. The same pundits who see the social safety net fraying under the weight of the retiring boomers are also observing that those retiring boomers are an enormous storehouse of workplace knowledge, skills, and experience. Our employers are going to miss us when we're gone! In fact, there are credible predictions that Canada will experience a severe shortage of skilled labor, both intellectual and manual, when the boomers retire.

That gives us a lot of bargaining power. If your employer can't replace you when you leave, you can set the terms of your departure. If you don't want to stay full time, he or she may be happy enough to keep you on a part-time basis. Some employers are even implementing formal "phased retirement" programs to encourage employees to stay in their jobs, scaling back their time commitments as a transitional measure. So if a part-time version of your full-time career is what you want, don't hesitate to approach your employer and ask for it. What's the worst that can happen? If the boss says no, you can move on to another option. If the boss says yes, it may be a happy solution all round.

A word of warning, though. If you're a member of an employee pension plan and you're considering cutting back to part-time work, check out whether you can still contribute to the plan. Your employer may have separate plans for full-and part-time employees, and you may encounter financial penalties for switching from one to the other. In some cases, part-time work may not improve your pension benefits. In fact, under plans with a benefit formula based on your salary in the *last* few years of your employment (a "last-years" formula), as opposed to the *best* few years of employment (a "best-years" formula), going part time and reducing your salary may drag your benefit down. Access to other non-pension retirement benefits may also be affected by part-time status. Ask for specific advice on the terms of your pension plan. If you're the pioneer in your company, you may have to negotiate some of these issues in order to ensure that you won't be permanently penalized for moving from full to part time. Check your collective agreement, if you're lucky enough to have one. If your union has negotiated a formal "phased retirement" program, it's likely that benefit penalties that might operate as disincentives to transitional pre-retirement employment have been eliminated.

There is one other issue to consider if you're weighing the pros and cons of continuing to work for your old employer. If you're currently eligible to collect pension benefits from your employer's plan, you may have to choose between collecting the pension and continuing in the job. The legal rules about this are complicated, and they may be about to change somewhat as a result of proposals in the March 2007 federal budget. But these changes aren't law yet, as we go to press. Before you try this, get advice! Working while you're collecting pension won't be a problem at all if you're working for a different employer. So depending on the terms of your pension plan, you may be financially better off to retire, take your pension, and peddle your skills to another employer, so you can collect a salary and a pension at the same time.

FINDING ANOTHER JOB

Maybe you don't want to stay at your current job a moment longer than you originally planned, even part time. And maybe you can't, either because you've been "down-sized" or because technological change or restructuring has turned your workplace into an alien planet. What then?

Same Career, Different Employer

Here's another option: change your job. If it's your current workplace you don't like, not your work, take a look around for something in the same field somewhere else. Not all jobs, even in the same profession, are alike.

Check around. Talk to your fellow professionals. Maybe you loved the fast pace at your workplace when you were younger and brasher and hungrier, but it's just not for you anymore. There's bound to be something more sustainable out there in the career you love. Just because you're a lawyer doesn't mean that you have to work a seventy-hour week. You'll last longer working in a legal aid clinic than you will on Bay Street. And you might just enjoy it more! If you're a teacher, you may find a private school or a tutoring center more tranquil than the public school system these days, and more amenable to letting you design your own schedule. If you're a nurse, burned out by twelve-hour shifts, maybe you should try public health, or agency nursing.

"Retiree" Jobs

The archetype of the low-stress, post-retirement job is the Wal-Mart Greeter — the peppy senior citizen who brightens your day when you walk into your local mega-discount store with a cheerful "How are the kiddies today?" and then offers clear, concise directions to the aisle display for the advertised special on laundry soap. There are lots of these jobs

Every year the Canadian Association of Retired People (CARP) honors top employers of Canadians over 50. In 2005, honorees from all across the country included :

- The Catholic Children's Aid Society of Toronto
- The City of Calgary
- Direct Energy
- Excell Services, Penticton, BC
- Merck Frosst, Montreal
- Seven Oaks General Hospital, Winnipeg

In prior years, winners have included Avis Rent-A-Car, RBC Royal Bank and, of course, The Home Depot.

(even if your community is lucky enough to lack a Wal-Mart!). Many tap into the expertise you built up in your pre-retirement job — The Home Depot is an example much touted in the Sunday newspaper articles on the post-retirement work phenomenon. There are also jobs that allow you to explore hobbies and interests you never had enough time to pursue while you were working — jobs at the local golf course are much sought after by retirees. These jobs don't usually pay much, but they're easy to find and older workers are sought and valued. They're more likely to be flexible about allowing time off. And if they aren't, you can always quit and pick up another one when the grandchildren go back to school in the fall or you get back from that dream trip to Australia.

Launching a New Career

Maybe half measures won't do — you want a real change. And maybe you're not just looking for a little extra pocket money and a reason to get out of the house. You're thinking *big*. You're thinking that you put thirty years into your last career, and there's another good thirty years in the old girl yet. You see NOW as your chance to follow that road not taken, stretch yourself, pursue that dream you set aside when you decided to go into teaching, or law, or the health professions.

Refurbishing Your Skill Set

If your dream career requires you to get more education or training, do it! University and college programs accept older students. They may even prefer older students, who are less likely to get hooked on drugs or have nervous breakdowns or forget to hand in their term papers. Art schools, drama schools, writing workshops, computer colleges — all of these would be happy to hear from you. Both graduate and undergraduate programs in the liberal arts welcome mature students of all ages. Professional schools may be more intimidating to older students, but human rights laws protect you from age discrimination in admissions, so if what you've always wanted is to be a physician or a lawyer, by all means apply if you qualify (and can afford the extortionate tuition fees!). And you'll have one advantage your younger classmates don't have. You probably have a financial cushion, a bit of money set aside to live on while you're studying. You won't face the prospect of hauling a $60,000 student loan around for years after you graduate.

Applying for That New Job

Maybe your dream career doesn't require any further education or training — maybe all it requires is the courage to polish up your resume and apply. It's a daunting thought, like being back in the dating game after a long marriage. All the rules seem to have changed since the last time you were out there, and your abs aren't flat anymore, and your hair seems to have turned grey and lost its bounce. But remember our little lesson in demography. If you've got skills to offer, they need you out there!

There are agencies that specialize in assisting older women to re-enter the workforce. Maybe that's you — if you've been out of the workforce or working part time while you raised a family, you may only now be figuring out what you want to do. But even if that isn't you, even if you've had a full-time career, you've still got some characteristics in common with women who stayed home. Your secure job protected you from the rough and tumble of looking for work. Unless you've worked in human resources, you won't know the current job-hunt buzz words. You may not have updated your resumé for thirty years. Even if you were completely self-confident in your old job, you may still be insecure about your ability to tackle a whole new field. If you live in Ontario, you can check out the websites for Times Change (www.timeschange.org) and ACTEW (it stands for A Commitment to Training and Employment for Women, www.actew.org), two organizations that provide useful services and information for older women hunting for jobs.

Skillsmatch is a job-hunting website for older Canadians. In addition to job postings, it offers some self-assessment tools for a fee. The unique feature of this service is that you can e-mail the result of your tests and your resumé to prospective employers who have listed jobs on Skillsmatch. Check it out at www.skillsmatch.ca, or access it through the CARP website: www.50plus.com.

WORKING YOUR WAY AROUND THE WORLD
Jobs in Other Countries

Lots of retirees want to travel the world. If this is your dream, but you can't afford it on your projected retirement income, even by employing strategies like house-swapping and traveling off season, working abroad may be an exciting way to slake your wanderlust while putting a little money in your pocket. Working in a foreign country is also a popular option for people who want to take a closer look at other lands and cultures than most tourists ever get.

Finding employment in foreign countries isn't easy, no matter how extensive your skills. Most countries do not encourage citizens of other countries to come in, either short term or long term, and take work opportunities they would rather reserve for their own nationals. (Canada, of course, follows this policy as well.) Tight controls on immigration and visa/work permits can be difficult barriers to surmount. But there are opportunities for those who have the persistence to pursue them.

The Canadian government puts out a publication, *Working Abroad: Unravelling the Maze*, downloadable from the federal government's Consular Affairs website at www.voyage.gc.ca (look under "Publications"). It's jam-packed with useful information for Canadians considering work abroad, and while it doesn't answer all the questions by any means, it does provide useful direction about where to find the answers. Another must-read for Canadians considering working abroad is *What in the World is Going On*, also free on the Internet at www. destineducation.ca (click on "Canadian Students" and go all the way to the bottom of the screen for a downloadable version). This forty-page booklet, a publication of the Canadian Institute for International Education, is a readable, realistic and very practical guide to the pros, cons, and mechanics of seeking work and study opportunities abroad.

There are also a variety of websites available that list international job postings. One worth clicking on is www.transitionsabroad.com. Many of their specific job listings are more suitable for the younger crowd — summer jobs and jobs for *au pairs*, for example — but the site has lots of links to resources on how to find and prepare for longer-term work opportunities abroad in a variety of professions. Another site with more specific job listings is www.jobsabroad.com.

Teaching in International Schools

Even if immigration rules were not so restrictive, many Canadian professionals would have difficulty finding work in their field overseas because their professional credentials simply aren't portable. One important exception is teaching. Unlike lawyers, doctors, and other professionals, teachers are often able to move between English-speaking countries with relative ease. And even in non-English-speaking countries, there are often private schools for English-speaking students in expatriate communities. Retired teachers with Canadian certification have found work in France, Italy, and other European countries, as well as in many Asian countries, teaching a wide variety of subjects. One website worth checking out is www.teachabroad.com, which contains job postings for English-speaking teachers in many different countries of the world. Another useful site is www.tieonline.com, run by TIE-International Educator, a non-profit organization created to assist international schools in finding English-speaking teachers. TIE's online job posting service is restricted to subscribers, at a cost of US$33 a year, but the website is worth a visit even if you don't subscribe. Keep your eyes open for international job fairs as well — Queen's University in Kingston, Ontario, for example, hosts an annual Teachers' Overseas Recruiting Fair that is attended by recruiters from international schools.

These positions are different from international teacher exchanges — you're retired now, so you have no position to exchange. They are usually less well paid (and in return, they are usually less demanding). But they'll get you to interesting foreign countries and pay your expenses while you're there.

Teaching ESL

Even if you don't have a teaching certificate, teaching English abroad is a feasible and very popular option. English is now the language of global commerce, and governments and businesses all around the world are scrambling to meet the need to train their citizens and employees in basic, conversational, and specialized business English. There is a virtually unlimited market for native English speakers (and others fluent in English) to teach English as a Second Language (ESL) to children, to adolescents, and in particular to adults.

Teaching ESL well requires more than the ability to speak English. And teaching adults is also a specialized skill in and of itself. Most reputable and well-paying employers require some evidence that you have acquired the skills necessary to teach ESL, usually in the form of a TESL or TESOL certificate.

There is no universal international standard for a TESL certificate, and many of the certificates that are available are quite easy to come by — for a price. It's buyer beware in shopping around for ESL teacher training. Instruction is offered by universities and community colleges, with programs ranging from two weeks to a full academic year. Courses are also offered by a host of private companies, some of whom claim you can qualify in five days, as well as through online or correspondence courses. If you're interested, try to get references from people who have actually taken these programs. If you know where you want to work and who you want to work for, find out what certification that government or employer recognizes. Many ESL jobs can be had with no certification at all, although these tend to be at the dodgier schools or tutoring agencies, and such assignments will not be as well paid.

ESL teaching can pay well, and is often attractive to recent graduates, who, if they play their cards right, can live cheaply abroad and put money aside to pay off student loans. The better-paid teachers work hard for their higher salaries, however, and you may be content with lower pay in return for a job that's less labor-intensive, especially if what you want is free time to enjoy another culture, learn a language, or just relax on a beach every afternoon. Be careful of what commitments you make. Many employers offer free airfare in return for a one-year contract, but if you don't find the job to your satisfaction, you're on your own, so make sure you have a valid return ticket or enough money tucked away to get back home.

If you're interested in investigating teaching English abroad, there are numerous websites listing programs and opportunities. Just enter "teaching abroad" in your search engine. The federal government's Consular Affairs website offers useful downloadable pamphlets on teaching English in Korea, Taiwan, and Japan (www.voyage.gc.ca). And as always, remember there's no substitute for talking with someone who's actually been there. If you can't connect directly with a Canadian retired teacher who has been there and done that, try searching for relevant Internet chat boards. People who have had interesting experiences are usually more than willing to talk about them, whether they've been good or bad.

Women Working Abroad

Working abroad raises special issues for women. Canadian women still have a way to go to achieve full equality in our own society, but compared to women in many other countries in the world, let's face it — we have it pretty good. Most of us haven't experienced anything like the pervasive gender discrimination that exists in the countries we may be thinking of visiting. Women traveling or living alone will encounter material dangers that men do not face. In many countries, women do not appear in public unveiled, do not work outside the home, and do not even go out alone to shop. Think about these issues before seeking employment in any country that has a poor record for its treatment of women. Life there could be difficult, demoralizing, and dangerous for you, even if, as a foreign woman, you get special treatment. In some countries, staying inside a gated enclave for foreign nationals may be the only safe and practical option for women. And that's probably not the kind of cross-cultural experience you're looking for. Ask lots of questions of prospective employers. Talk to other women who have had experience working in the country you're interested in.

The Canadian government has issued a booklet, *Her Own Way: Advice for the Woman Traveller*, discussing issues of safety, health, and culture shock unique to women traveling. You can download a copy of this publication at www.voyage.gc.ca. One useful suggestion it offers is to seek out women now living in Canada who come from the country you are interested in visiting, and find out from them what life is really like for women in their homeland. The fact that a country discriminates against women is not, in itself, a reason not to go there; if that were our only criterion, we wouldn't get out much! But some choices are definitely worse than others, and it's important — indeed, it can be life-saving — to know what to expect.

CHAPTER 10

Your Own Boss

SELF-EMPLOYMENT: RISKS AND REWARDS

Many people in their fifties and sixties see retirement as an opportunity to start a small business of their own, either to follow a dream, or simply to keep an income stream flowing. It could be a cottage industry like home baking. It could be that mom-and-pop bookstore-and-cappuccino-bar you've always wished was in your neighborhood. It could be a large manufacturing enterprise. There's no limit except your interests, your energy level, your available capital — and your risk tolerance.

That last factor is an important one. It's a tough world out there, especially for those of us who have been sheltered by secure employment all our working lives. When you start a small business, you'll need solid, practical advice about the potential risks and rewards. Your personal assets — your retirement nest egg — will very likely be on the line. Don't count on your friendly neighborhood chartered bank to make you a loan unless you've got collateral to back up your business plan. Your business idea may be spectacular, but if it goes bust, the bank wants to ensure that *you* are the one to take the fall.

So before you sign anything, ponder this sobering statistic: Almost 10,000 Canadian businesses filed for bankruptcy in 2005. A lot of these were business start-ups — people with great ideas just like yours, who couldn't make a go of it. Success comes to the risk-takers, to be sure, but if you're thinking of a venture that will require a substantial capital investment, be sure you have a comprehensive and prudent business plan in place.

We aren't saying any of this to discourage you. If you're prepared to do your homework and take some risks, starting your own business can be very profitable and very satisfying. But be careful!

NUTS AND BOLTS OF STARTING A SMALL BUSINESS

There's lots of information available on the Internet for Canadians considering starting a small business. The BC government website, www.bcbusinessregistry.ca, is a particularly rich treasure trove of information for small business neophytes, with a wealth of useful links. You can click on #1 on the home page, "Information on Starting Your Business" to download the booklet, *Starting a Small Business in British Columbia*, and then link directly to www.smallbusinessbc.ca. Once you get there, clicking on "Guides and Websites" will take you to useful information about a variety of specific small businesses, like bed-and-breakfasts, ecotourism, franchises, consulting, and many more. While some of the legal information on these websites applies only to British Columbia, they are a useful resource for women in other provinces as well. Ontario's recently created Ministry of Small Business and Entrepreneurs (www.sbe.gov.on.ca) offers a downloadable copy of an Ontario-focused publication, *Your Guide to Small Business*. You should also check out Ontario's Business Start-up Assistant. Go to www.gov.on.ca, click on "Business" on the left-hand, and choose "Assistant" from the menu. You'll then be offered links to all the information you'll need to think through your business plan, deal with financing, choose a business structure, register the business, hire employees, and comply with a variety of legal requirements for running a business. For federal government resources for Canadians thinking about starting a small business, visit www.canada.gc.ca. Click on "Canada Business," and then on "Starting a Business."

Business Structure

If you don't have any business background, you may need some advice to help you set things up. It's not as hard as it looks. A business can be run as a sole proprietorship, a partnership (either limited or unlimited), a professional corporation, or an ordinary corporation. The government websites referred to above will give you the basics on these options, and both the federal and provincial governments have business advisory services (for contact information, check the websites). Business how-to books are also useful (see Further Reading for this chapter), and the business pages of your local newspaper may list one-day or weekend seminars on the basics, run by the government or the business community. Check your local school board or community college continuing education program listings as well if you need more help.

If you're thinking about a home-based business, you won't want or need to get too fancy. The benefits of keeping it simple — a sole proprietorship (just you, unincorporated) or a partnership (you and your spouse, or you and a friend who are going into business together) — will outweigh the tax advantages of the more complex structures. If your business is risky (e.g., you want to lead adventure tours to Afghanistan), you may want to incorporate to get limited liability protection (i.e. protection from personal liability) in conducting the business, as well as lots of insurance.

Business Names

If your "company" is just you, under your own name, you don't need to register with the government to run a business. You just need to pay your taxes on time. But if you are going to be operating under a business name — for example "My Name Consulting" or "Aardvark Ideas," you need to register your business name. A partnership name is considered a business name, so if you're going into business with someone else and you plan to call yourself "Jekyll & Hyde" or "J&H Associates," you need to register.

It's easy, and relatively inexpensive. If you live in Ontario, you can register online for a fee of $60, which gives you a license to operate for five years. Just go to www.gov.on.ca. Click on "Business" on the left-hand side, and follow the links to ServiceOntario, where you can register your new business. Likewise the British Columbia government provides an excellent "one-stop shopping" website for small business, www.bcbusinessregistry.ca, where you can register your unincorporated small business for a fee of $40, and link to other relevant sites to register for things like GST (see below). In BC, you need prior approval of your business name before you can register. You can't get this online yet, but you can obtain a copy of the mail-in form on the business registry website.

Most other provinces also offer web registration services — search the provincial government websites for the links you need in your province.

GST

If you don't aspire to bill over $30,000 in any one tax year, you don't need to collect GST from your clients, and you don't need to register for GST. If you're planning to do more business than that, you need to register and get a GST number. You can do that online as well, and it's free. Go to www.canada.gc.ca. Click on "Canada Business," then "Starting a Business," then "Business Startup Assistant." Then select the province in which you'll be starting your business.

When you get there, you'll find out that if you live in Ontario,

New Brunswick, Nova Scotia, or British Columbia, you could have saved yourself a step. For those provinces, the federal government website offers you the option of doing a combined GST/Provincial Business Name registration, all with one set of forms, and one set of clicks. You'll pay only the fee your province requires for business name registration, since the GST registration is free.

Even if you don't *have* to register for GST, there are reasons why you might *want* to. Clients and customers are used to paying GST, so you probably won't get much of a business edge by not charging it. And you're labeling yourself a micro-business if you don't — you may not want your clients to know you don't do enough business to charge GST. In addition, if you collect GST, you can also get credit for any GST you pay on business supplies and services. The paperwork for dealing with GST isn't terribly onerous — if you do less than $500,000 worth of taxable business, you only have to report once a year — so you might want to consider it.

And for smaller service businesses, the government provides a simplified Quick Method process that eliminates the necessity of balancing "input" and "output" GST credits. This means that you don't need to keep track of the GST you pay on business expenses and subtract it from the GST you collect before remitting it to the government. If you're interested in using the Quick Method, obtain a copy of the booklet *Quick Method of Accounting for GST/HST* by calling 1-800-959-2221, or view it on the website. New businesses who want to take advantage of the Quick Method should register right away. You can do this by phone at the number above. You can change your election about what method you want to use prior to the beginning of any new reporting period.

The federal government also provides workshops and seminars on GST for small businesses. Call 1-800-959-2221 for information about scheduling and locations, or check the website.

Record-Keeping for Tax Purposes

While registering for GST is optional for micro-businesses, paying income tax isn't optional for any of us. Income tax must be paid, and it must be paid on time. Proper business records must be maintained to ensure that you're doing this properly.

You pay tax only on your *net* income, of course. To arrive at your net income, you calculate your total revenues, and deduct appropriate business expenses (money you spent to earn that income). What's left is what you pay tax on.

Business Expenses

What are appropriate business expenses? The answer varies depending on the nature of your business, so that's an issue you should take up with your accountant. As a general rule, though, we can't emphasize too much the importance of careful record keeping of *all* revenues and expenses. Keep track of your invoices, and make sure they get paid. Keep track of your receipts — for transportation (like gas, parking, and transit fares), for office supplies (like paper and postage), for business promotion (like taking your client out to lunch to discuss a new project or celebrate the successful completion of an old one). If you don't keep proper track of your revenues and expenses, you'll have a very hard time justifying your deductions. And that can be an expensive problem to have.

The Canada Revenue Agency has a number of useful publications on income tax issues for small businesses, and in particular on the issue of home office expenses. Have a look at:

RC4070: Guide for Canadian Small Business
T4002: Business and Professional Income
IT-514: Work Space in Home Expenses

These publications are all available online at the CRA website (www.cra-arc.gc.ca) under "Forms and Publications," or from local tax offices.

It's easier to keep track of business revenues and expenses if you maintain separate bank accounts and separate credit cards for your business. It can be a bit of a hassle to set these up, but it's inexpensive and it's worth it. It keeps things on track, and it also goes a long way to convincing the Canada Revenue Agency that you're really running a business and not just trying to hoodwink the taxpayers into subsidizing a hobby. Letterhead and business cards help too.

Home Office Expenses

One of the attractions of a home-based business is the opportunity — and it's perfectly legal — to write off some of the expenses of running your home. Mortgage payments or rent, utilities, cleaning, Internet fees, property taxes, even the costs of landscaping and gardening, are all deductible expenses as long you can attribute them to the earning of business revenues.

You can't be too greedy here. The tax rules permit you to characterize a reasonable proportion of the costs of running and maintaining your house as business expenses. The key word is "reasonable." If your home office is tucked away in a corner of your basement, don't try to deduct half your costs. Measure the office, and figure out what percentage of the total square footage of your house the office occupies. If it's 10 percent, deduct 10 percent of your home operating expenses. If you use the room as an office during the day, but it's the TV room at night (and you actually watch TV!), cut your deduction back proportionately. And if the cost of your home office consistently exceeds the revenue from your business, you can expect some questions about whether you're really in business to make money — the only motivation the tax department recognizes as legitimate. The tax department doesn't like "lifestyle businesses," and you may find some of your deductions slashed or disallowed.

Income Tax

Just like employees, business people have to pre-pay their income taxes. After the first year of self-employment, taxes on business income have to be pre-paid in quarterly instalments. Calculating those instalments can feel a bit haphazard. You're paying in advance, so you have to estimate how much you'll earn this year, and divide it by four. Earnings are almost always more unpredictable for the self-employed than for the employed. If you estimate wrong and pay too much, you'll get it back. If you pay too little, however, you'll have to pay some interest.

The most hassle-free method of paying income tax instalments is online through your bank's website. If you already use web banking, all you need to set up online instalment payments is your social insurance number. There are other ways to pay, of course, if you're not comfortable with moving money around on the web. Call CRA, or consult your accountant.

BUSINESS IDEAS

Sources of Business Ideas

The best business ideas are the ones you think of yourself — but if you need some suggestions to get the juices flowing, there are lots of "idea" books out there. We've listed several of these in the Further Reading section for this chapter at the back of the book. There are also lots of books that will help you develop your business plan for whatever you have in mind: restaurants, call centres, landscaping, bookkeeping, laundromats, desktop publishing, crafts, event planning, tour-guiding, selling antiques — you name it, and somebody's written a book about how to turn it into a successful business.

And just consider the demographics. The wave of retiring boomers will produce a wave of new entrepreneurs. But it will also create new needs and new markets, and with them a wave of new business ideas for serving those needs and those markets. Here are some areas we've identified from our own research where the needs and wants of retiring boomers appear currently to be under-serviced, or not serviced at all, in Canada:

- Travel services for retirees, both singles and couples
- Information and counseling services on housing for retirees
- Property maintenance services for retirees who travel
- Career counseling for retirees and prospective retirees
- Services coordinating volunteer opportunities for retirees
- Fitness facilities and sports programs for older women
- Weight management and nutritional advice for older women
- Services providing advice and assistance with the care of elderly parents
- Services providing advice and assistance on modifying existing homes to accommodate physical limitations
- Domestic and personal care services for retirees.

Consulting

One popular small business for retirees is consulting. "Consulting" is a very capacious term with a wide variety of meanings. For new retirees, it often means continuing to do what you have always done, but on a freelance basis rather than as an employee or partner/associate of an established business. Often (although not always) the key client for a new consultant is a former employer.

In theory, consulting work gives retirees the best of both worlds. You can continue to use tried-and-true skills, in return for compensation at levels similar to those you were earning in your career jobs. In fact, if your skills are particularly marketable you can sometimes make a better deal as a consultant than you can as an employee. This can happen if there's a real skill shortage in your particular line of work, or you've developed a specialization that will be difficult to replicate, or you're just particularly good at your job. As a consultant, you'll be able to work as much or as little as you're comfortable with. Consultants can take two months off in the summer, and give themselves breaks between projects. Consultants can say no to projects that don't interest them. They can say no to overwork.

That's in theory. In practice, of course, it doesn't always work out like that. Consultants can't be unavailable too often if they work in a competitive marketplace. If you turn down their key projects, clients will look for others who can meet their needs, and they may not have work for you when you need it. And unless you work hard at nurturing relationships with new clients, you may discover — sad to say — that your contacts dry up as the people you worked with retire themselves or move on.

The Property Business

Another area that interests many retirees is property investment. Some seek rental properties to generate an income stream; they're primarily interested in becoming landlords. Others seek to buy property that will appreciate in value, in hopes of selling it down the road for a profit. They're primarily investors or speculators. These categories are not mutually exclusive, of course. Many investors who buy condos with capital appreciation in view will become landlords while they're waiting, renting to tenants. And landlords also hope to make capital gains down the road when they sell. In other words, they're also investors. But even though the categories overlap, it is important to be very clear on your primary objectives before you embark on property-buying ventures.

Being a landlord isn't as simple as it looks. Just because a house is good value for a homeowner doesn't mean it's good value for a landlord. When considering the purchase of a potential rental property, you need to consider carefully whether you can rent it out easily and keep it tenanted. You'll be looking for long-term tenants, if possible. If you choose well-located properties and keep them well maintained, you can probably keep them tenanted most of the time. But some vacancy periods are almost inevitable — rental markets have their ebbs and flows. If you need regular rental income to pay the mortgage, you could run into trouble if a landlords' market suddenly turns into a tenants' market.

You also need to consider whether the rent you can charge will be enough to pay all your expenses and also generate some profit. Expenses may be more than you expect. Maintenance is part of the normal responsibility of a landlord, and it costs money. You can't ask your tenants to make do until you can afford to fix something, the way you might in your own home in a pinch. If you've cultivated some practical skills yourself, you can keep maintenance costs down. But if you've never been handy — and as women, we were conditioned to leave all this to our menfolk — a lot of your profit can bleed away in paying tradespeople to fix the plumbing and patch the roof and get rid of the squirrels in the attic. Some big landlords contract out all of these headaches to property management companies. But if you're a small landlord, you will probably find management fees eating up all your profits. So you'll have to be prepared to invest time as well as money in the business.

If you're investing in property in the hope of capital appreciation, you need to do your research very thoroughly, and you need good advice from experts who aren't just trying to make a quick buck off your inexperience. It's tempting, when the housing market just seems to go up and up and up, to try to get in on the ride. But history shows us that it doesn't always go up and up and up. We've been around long enough to have seen dramatic downturns as well. In Canada's major cities, those who bought at the crest of the wave in the later 1980s had to hold on to their houses for more than ten years even to recover their investment. Those forced to sell before prices recovered lost money, and many speculators who counted on quick capital gains went bankrupt when the value of their properties fell below the value of their mortgages. So take care!

Renting Out the Family Assets

In Chapter 7, we looked at the potential for renting out part of your family home — a room or a basement apartment — as an alternative to downsizing. That's an excellent example of how you can turn an income-depleting liability into a revenue-producing asset, in order to preserve those aspects of your lifestyle that you really value for as long as you can.

You can do the same thing with the family cottage, if you own one. While you were working, you used it maybe four weeks a year, and a few weekends. Now that you're retired, you'll be there more often than that, of course. But when it's vacant, remember that others might enjoy it too. It's a beautiful place and you're lucky to own it. Share it, and earn some income at the same time. Check the Internet for inexpensive listing agencies you can tap into to find reliable renters. Use your personal networks — you'd be surprised how many people want to enjoy a piece of the Canadian wilderness without having to buy it themselves. Don't forget that income from renting out the cottage is taxable, and must be declared. But you'll be able to deduct a portion of the cottage expenses, costs that you have to pay anyway, like utility bills and property taxes, whether you rent it out or not. Again, as with home office expenses, the rule is reasonableness.

So far we've talked about renting out real property. But you can do the same thing with other assets as well (what the lawyers call "personal property"). You can rent out that expensive recreational vehicle. You can rent out your leaf blower or your tractor lawn mower. You can rent out anything there's a market for. Just remember that the rules are always the same. The money you make is income from property. It's taxable, and in return, you can deduct a reasonable portion of the costs of owning and operating the asset.

CHAPTER 11

Working For Love

"OUR" TIME

Retirement was never quite the wide ocean of discretionary time portrayed in those "Freedom Fifty-Five" ads that showed beautiful beaches and happy retired couples holding hands as they walked in the sunshine. Even without paid work, retirees have always had some of their work cut out for them. They still managed homes, tended families, managed their own finances, and looked after their health. New Retirees will have all of that to deal with, and women in particular, with their longer lives and longer retirements, will face financial challenges that may keep them doing some work for pay for longer than they anticipated.

But inevitably, our paid work will taper off as we get older. We will have increasing amounts of time that is "our" time. And we will be challenged to make satisfying use of that time.

The companies that currently market products and services to retirees often make the convenient and profitable assumption that retirement is playtime. If life were like the commercials, retirees who are free of financial constraints would pass their time buying second homes in warmer climates, making frequent long trips to five-star hotels in exotic locales, taking up costly recreational activities like golf and skiing, treating the grandchildren to trips to Disney World. Nice for a while, for those with that kind of dough. But even retirees who can afford it soon figure out that it takes more than play to make a life. They'll find themselves wanting to remain creative, productive, and engaged with the world. They need work as well as play.

We're all different, of course. Some of us will want to continue to make use of the skills we have already developed, the skills that ratify and affirm our sense of competence and mastery. Others see retirement as an opportunity to nurture aspects of themselves that were submerged throughout their working lives — their spirituality, their creativity, their sense of connection with the natural world or the community. They may launch environmental crusades, teach yoga, paint, or write. There aren't any off-the-shelf packages that will fit all needs. The important thing is to get to know ourselves again, to identify our own needs, to listen to our inner voices, and to plan for the work we will do in "our" time with as much care as we took in planning our careers.

In 2005, an Ipsos Reid survey asked men and women: "Ideally, how would you like to spend your time in retirement?" This chart shows selected responses to the question.

ACTIVITY	TOTAL	FEMALE	MALE
Recreation	**79%**	**86%**	**74%**
Traveling	58%	66%	54%
Spending time with family and friends	25%	35%	19%
Hobbies/Recreation/Crafts	12%	13%	12%
Gardening/Yard Work	10%	14%	7%
Reading	9%	13%	6%

Relaxing	9%	8%	9%
Working	**27%**	**30%**	**25%**
Volunteer Work	18%	23%	14%
Miscellaneous	**24%**	**27%**	**23%**
Doing activities I want to do	12%	11%	12%
Staying active	6%	8%	6%
Take up courses/learn new skills	4%	6%	3%
Sports	**14%**	**15%**	**13%**
Golfing	8%	5%	10%
Skiing	1%	1%	1%
Swimming	0%	1%	0%

Source: Ipsos Reid/BMO Bank of Montreal Survey on Retirement, December 7, 2005

Lots of variety out there. And no real surprises. But the responses do raise one rather alarming question: What on earth are *men* going to do in retirement? The women were enthusiastically embracing recreation, travel, spending time with family and friends, and doing volunteer work by a considerable margin over the men. The answers given by the men were considerably vaguer, and the only activities to which they responded more positively than the women by a margin of more than one percent were fishing (4 percent men, 1 percent women), sports (15 percent men, 13 percent women), and golfing (10 percent men, 5 percent women). Hardly a recipe for a full and satisfying life!

So what will we do with "our time"?

VOLUNTEERING

Working with charities and other non-profit organizations on worthy projects is a time-honored role for retirees. Many see it as a way of "giving back" to the community that nurtured their professional success. Others, less altruistic but perhaps more realistic, simply want to pursue new interests or make new friends. Whatever their initial motivation, retirees who take up volunteer work routinely report that they get back far more than they give. Significant numbers report improvements to communications, managerial and fund-raising skills, and to knowledge related to the area of volunteer activity.

Volunteers in Canada

There are more than 175,000 registered charities and non-profit organizations in Canada. Thousands of them operate on-going programs, and almost all of them are desperate for volunteers to carry out their work.

The term "non-profit" includes charities, but not all non-profits are eligible for registration as charities. To qualify for registration in Canada, which qualifies them to issue tax receipts for contributions, organizations must be engaged in activities that fall into one of four categories that date back to the sixteenth century: the relief of poverty; the advancement of education; the advancement of religion; and purposes beneficial to the community. While these categories are broad, there are all sorts of interesting institutions that don't fall under any of these headings. If the work of a non-profit interests you, don't be deterred from volunteering just because it's not registered as a charity.

Health care, education, religion, arts and culture, social services, human rights, animal rights, international development, support for children and the elderly, athletics, the environment, fighting poverty, running women's shelters — you name the issue, and you can almost certainly find an organization out there that needs your volunteer time badly. And it's not as hard as you might think to find a good match.

Large, established charities put a lot of time and effort into organizing the work of volunteers — if you call the executive director or volunteer coordinator you may find that they can train you and put you to work right away. Smaller organizations have less staff — some have no staff at all — and may be less experienced at using volunteers. They may not be able to fit you in immediately. But if you're persistent, you'll find a role (maybe as volunteer co-ordinator!).

Surprising as it sounds, some institutions don't need more volunteers. A large art galley or internationally acclaimed symphony orchestra may not greet your desire to help out with quite the warmth you think it deserves — there may be long waiting lists for volunteer positions. But if you're interested in the arts, don't despair. There are many small theater groups and arts and music festivals that need help. If your interest is in social services or health care, you may find that the volunteer quota has been met for the year at your large local hospital, or that the best volunteer opportunities go to the volunteers with "seniority." But a local shelter or helpline may be delighted to train you and assign you quite quickly to front-line work.

Smaller organizations aren't as well publicized, and that's where non-profit services like Volunteer Canada (with its local and regional links), Charity Village, and Board Match come in. These organizations all run websites with information about charities and non-profit organizations seeking volunteers. They're like job-posting services, only of course you don't get paid.

Some websites for prospective volunteers:

- **Charity Village**
  www.charityvillage.ca
  This website, which describes itself as "Canada's supersite for the non-profit sector," posts volunteer opportunities from all across the country. It also lists links to local volunteer centers across Canada, and paying positions in the non-profit sector.

- **Volunteer Canada**
  www.volunteercanada.ca

This site offers a self-assessment questionnaire to assist prospective volunteers to determine what opportunities they might be most suitable for. It also provides links to volunteer centers across the country that list specific volunteer opportunities and match volunteers up with organizations seeking volunteers.

- **Board Match Fundamentals**
www.boardmatch.org
This service, operated by the non-profit Altruvest Charitable Services, matches prospective volunteers with charities and non-profits seeking new board members. It currently lists organizations in the Greater Toronto Area, Dufferin, Halton, Peel, Durham, York Region, and in Greater Vancouver. The website provides online orientation and tutorials on issues of board governance.

- **Imagine Canada**
www.imaginecanada.ca
Imagine Canada is a national organization encouraging corporate and private charitable giving. Through its "Giving and Volunteering" section, this website provides links to a variety of organizations across the country serving volunteers and prospective volunteers.

Volunteers Abroad

We often think of volunteering outside the country as a young person's game. But the fact is that retirees are even more popular than young people as volunteers in many developing countries. They are mature. They know their own limits. They have acquired some cultural humility. They have skills, knowledge, and experience.

Legitimate non-governmental organizations (NGOs) often have very high standards for staffing overseas projects and are looking for specific skills, knowledge, and experience. If you check the website for the Canadian University Services Overseas (CUSO) (www.cuso.org), you'll find "job" postings asking for qualifications like MBAs and graduate degrees in psychology. Trained teachers are also in demand, as are health care professionals. NGOs don't have the time or the funds to provide much training for volunteers, so even if your labor is free, they'll always prefer someone who already has the skills over one who doesn't. But not all overseas organizations are so demanding. Some programs do not require special skills and expertise; Blyth Education, for example, which runs programs in Cuba, Ethiopia, and Tanzania, accepts volunteers with a broad range of backgrounds and life experience. For information on their programs, go to www.blytheducation.com and click on "The View Foundation."

One agency that specializes in placing older Canadians in volunteer assignments is the Canadian Executive Services Overseas. Their website (www.ceso-saco.com) advises that the average age of their volunteers is sixty-two. Check the website for Global Citizens for Change (www.citizens4change.org) for a listing of Canadian organizations that accept volunteers. Some of the listed organizations target young people in particular, but others accept useful volunteers from all age groups. If you're a teacher looking for volunteer opportunities, check out www.worldteach.org, a Harvard-based NGO in operation since 1986, which lists volunteer teaching opportunities all around the world.

These volunteer gigs aren't always cost-free, so look carefully at the terms of the arrangements. CUSO volunteers (called "cooperants") don't have to pay; they are provided with a basic living allowance, simple but reasonably secure accommodation for the volunteer and accompanying family members, as well as appropriate health benefits. Some NGOs, however, do charge volunteers a fee or require them to fund-raise as a condition of participation. Blyth Education, for example, requires volunteers to cover the cost of airfare and living expenses. This may not seem fair, but remember: these groups are charities. Their mission is to serve the people in the country in which they operate, not to provide satisfying retirement experiences for you. They've done a cost-benefit analysis, and they've determined that using volunteer labor only works if you pay your own way. They need to conserve their resources to provide the programs in which you can play a part. If the organization is legitimate, and the assignment an interesting one, it may be worth it. You'll find that in most cases, volunteering is still a much cheaper way to get a close look at another country than being a conventional tourist. And you're helping to change the world into the bargain!

LIFELONG LEARNING
Going Back to School

Some retirees go back to school because they need more education or training to pursue their dream post-retirement careers. For others it's unfinished business, a chance to attend university for the first time or complete a degree abandoned at an earlier stage in life. Some just want the personal growth that comes with learning a new language or a new skill. The benefits are enormous; recent research leaves little doubt that continually challenging our intellect is the best way to ensure that it stays supple and serviceable as we age. "Use it or lose it" is a maxim that applies to minds as well as to bodies.

Continuing education programs

If you're not concerned about getting a degree or a diploma, there are lots of courses you can take to learn new skills or brush up on old ones, to pursue intellectual interests, or just to have fun. If you're in this group, there is a rich menu of choices out there in all price ranges.

For courses at the inexpensive end of the continuum, check out non-commercial continuing education resources first:

- university courses targeted at alumni
- non-credit college and university courses targeted at retirees
- evening courses offered by local boards of education (less prevalent than they used to be after cutbacks to funding, but still available in some provinces)
- skills exchanges, in which volunteers offer courses in their area of interest and expertise (the Toronto version died, sadly, in the mid-'80s, but you may get lucky elsewhere)

Check notices posted on community bulletin boards and telephone poles, as well as your community newspapers, for ads and information about more informal courses offered in your neighborhood. And for commercial offerings, of which there are many, check ads in local newspapers, as well as the Yellow Pages or similar directories.

Travel-education programs

The best known travel-education program geared to retirees is Elderhostel, a U.S.-based non-profit organization providing educational travel to adults fifty-five and older in more than ninety countries worldwide. With Elderhostel you can work with marine biologists to study coral reefs in Belize, or do a Harry Potter tour of Oxford, England. You can go bird-watching in Iceland or learn Spanish in Mexico. The choices are myriad and the price is right — an average of US$115 a day, all inclusive, once you get to your destination.

Don't be deterred by the Elderhostel stereotypes. It's true, some of the patrons of Elderhostel *are* earnest retired academics in corduroy jackets and Birkenstocks. But there are also people just like you, looking for inexpensive food for the mind along with their travels. Check out their website: www.elderhostel.org. There is no membership fee. They'll send you their catalogue free of charge, and you pay for the programs you choose.

Routes to Learning Canada, based in Kingston, Ontario, is not as well known as Elderhostel, but provides similar programs. In fact, it's Elderhostel's Canadian provider. Its website, www.routestolearning. ca, lists a wide variety of excursions both in Canada and elsewhere in the world. It offers both Classic Journeys (scheduled and programmed tours featuring lectures and cultural events), and Discovery Journeys (for smaller and more active groups, which combine programming with independent excursions). Routes to Learning Canada also partners with a number of other institutions in Canada offering educational programming for older adults. Click on "Routes Community" on the home page to find links to these partners, many of which offer local educational programming geared towards retirees.

Recreational Travel

Travel figures prominently in the dreams of many retiring Canadians. A number of non-profit organizations cater to traveling seniors. A good place to start is CARP Travel (accessible at www.50plus.com). CARP Travel books tours and cruises, and features long-stay vacations in a variety of destinations worldwide. The website also contains links to informative articles and other travel information. Another useful general site is Alberta-based Seniorsgotravel.com (www.seniorsgotravel.com), packed with tips and information about travel for older Canadians. The Canadian Snowbirds Association has a useful online magazine for seniors, *Lifestyle*, available on its website (www.snowbirds.org), and also sells its own travel medical insurance.

If price is less important to you than adventure, Seniors Tours Canada (www.seniorstours.ca), a commercial agency, offers guided tours to more conventional tourist destinations, and Eldertreks (www. eldertreks.com), billing itself as a luxury travel company, will arrange much more exotic (and more expensive) packages to glamorous and out-of-way destinations. Many agencies targeting the over-fifty crowd offer a choice between more sedentary travel, and adventure tours for the more active traveler who wants to go someplace her friends and neighbors haven't already been. Organized and guided tours come at a wide range of prices, so buyer beware! Check very carefully what's included in the price; some of these tours require you to pay your own return airfare from home to a pick-up point. It can sometimes be difficult to find discount flights to out-of-the-way destinations at convenient times.

Maybe you don't want a group — you'd rather go off on your own. If money is no object, it's likely that any good travel agent can find you what you want. If you're looking for bargains, however — and let's face it, most retirees are — you may have to be creative. Discount airfares and house-swapping opportunities help (we discussed these in Chapter 6), and you should also consult the guides the twentysomething backpackers use. You won't find *Europe on $5 a Day* anymore, but the publishers of the *Let's Go* guidebooks offer a series, *Let's Go … on a Budget*, which are inexpensive, well written, entertaining and useful for travelers of any age looking for local bargains at a chosen destination. The *Lonely Planet* also publishes its *On a Shoestring* series for budget travelers: These guides cost more than the *Let's Go* guides, but are a little more user-friendly. The *Independent Traveller* series of budget guides is also well worth a look. Be realistic, though. You're not twenty any more, and you may find that sacrifices you were willing to make on your first backpack trip to Europe aren't nearly as much fun as they used to be. Remember you're traveling for pleasure. If cockroaches make your skin crawl, if your back aches all day after you sleep on a lumpy mattress, a fleabag hotel won't be a good choice for you even if you save lots of money.

Women without partners may wonder if traveling alone is too much of a risk. But it may actually be safer and easier for you now than it was when you were younger. Your age commands respect and buys you at least some immunity from the notion prevailing in many countries that women on their own are sexual prey. Certainly many women do travel alone, live to tell the tale, and report enormous satisfaction. Foreign Affairs Canada's publication, *Her Own Way: Advice for the Woman Traveller* advises some common sense precautions for all ages. You can get a copy on the Consular Affairs website at www.voyage.gc.ca. You should also check out www.journeywomen.com, a site that describes itself as the "Premier Travel Resource for Women." Make sure you click on "The Older Adventuress," for entertaining and informative articles about travel for older women, including useful tips on travel bargain hunting. And don't forget to re-read the section on "Women Working Abroad" in Chapter 9; there's good advice there even for casual tourists in countries that are known as unfriendly to women.

It may be more expensive to travel alone than with a partner. You won't be able to take advantage of the economies of double rooms, and you may be charged a single's supplement at some resorts and on some package tours. If that's a concern, or you just want some company, you might want to consider services available to match women up with other women going alone to the same destination. CARP's affiliated web-site, www.50plus.com, offers a link to www.travelaquaintance.com, which for a small fee offers to match up single travelers with others of like mind interested in the same destinations.

Hobbies

> *Hobby*: "a pursuit outside one's regular occupation engaged in especially for relaxation"
> Merriam Webster Online Dictionary

The word "hobby" has had a bad rap. When we think of hobbies, we think of puttering — useless but time-consuming activities designed to keep dad out of the kitchen while mum makes dinner. In fact, all that distinguishes a hobby from a job is that it's undertaken for fun rather than for remuneration. Hobbies are the things we choose to do, rather than the things we have to do. Hobbies, therefore, are quintessentially appropriate activities if we're looking for satisfying ways to use "our" time.

If you don't have a hobby, choose one! There are lots of creative activities you can try — how about ballroom dancing, throwing pots, playing the flute, or fabric art? — and fascinating items to collect, like antiques or rare books. Maybe now's the time to write that family history. Maybe you want to get serious about Scrabble or chess. Maybe you want to attend a Star Trek convention. Or you might want to read up on some special topic in art or science that has always piqued your imagination. You can do these things alone, or join a group or club.

If you need some ideas to get you started, there are lots of resources to help you find out about the vast range of hobbies that have engaged other Canadians. Browsing the Craft, Hobby, or Do-it-Yourself sections of any big bookstore will get your juices flowing. There are often craft and hobby markets, trade shows, fairs, and conventions in major cities, and hobby shops in smaller centers. These venues are full of enthusiasts looking for new recruits to their own passions; once you decide to narrow your choices, you shouldn't have much difficulty finding help along the way.

Sports and Athletics

Sports and athletics have always been popular pastimes for Canadians. Older Canadians, however, are less active than they should be. That's a shame. And it's also unhealthy. The research is in now — there's no question that the fitter we are, the longer we'll live, and the better we'll enjoy life. So if you're not active now, you should seriously consider changing that.

There are many kinds of sporting activities tailored to different aptitudes, activity levels, and pocketbooks. The 2005 Ipsos Reid survey identified golf as the primary sports interest of prospective Canadian retirees — no surprise there! Swimming and skiing also attracted some adherents. But there are older Canadians engaged in all manner of sporting activities. Your general fitness and level of conditioning — or just common sense! — may steer you away from some of the more extreme sports, but age itself need be no barrier to participation in any sport on the planet.

In view of the current public policy interest in getting seniors more active, there are surprisingly few resources out there specifically targeted to the older athlete. It's not easy to track down organized athletic activities that address the needs of older adults, and in particular older women. The Ontario Government's Active 2010 program is designed to get Ontarians off their butts, but it has very little of specific interest to the older adult. Its website (www.active2010.ca) allows you to search for organizations offering specific athletic activities in your town, city, or region. For example, a search for "skating" in the Greater Sudbury Region offers thirteen different arenas, with links to their websites. The Alberta Government does somewhat better; its Alberta Centre for Active Living offers a lengthy list of resources for getting seniors more involved in sports and athletics. Visit www.centre4activeliving.ca, and select "Older adults" from the "Populations" menu. There are, of course, the Canada Seniors Games, a venue for older athletes to compete against each other in activities ranging from lawn bowling to Alpine skiing (and including duplicate bridge!). Consult the website of the Canada Senior Games Association for links to provincial associations (www.canada55plusgames.com). But there's not much out there for women who want simply to play, not to compete. And that's a shame too!

Sports for older adults is an issue whose time has come. In fact, if you're looking for a project to get involved in, why not consider organizing a volleyball, basketball, or badminton league — or whatever you fancy — for older women in your locale.

Just do it!

Health Matters

Most people do not realize that throughout the history of life on earth, aging has been an exceedingly rare phenomenon. The natural world is, and always has been, a hostile place in which the vast majority of organisms die before they have an opportunity to grow old.

S. Jay Olshansky and Bruce A. Carnes, *The Quest for Immortality: Science at the Frontiers of Aging*, New York: W.W. Norton & Co., 2001

COMING TO TERMS WITH AGING

Women of the generation that is now contemplating retirement have a hard time coming to terms with aging. We're boomers, after all. We've transformed every stage of life we've been through so far, and we expect to transform this one too. We understand, at an intellectual level, that death comes to us all in the end. But we plan to stay healthy for a long time to come. We have seen enormous advances in medical science in our lifetime, and we expect that by the time heart disease or cancer or Alzheimer's comes looking for us, there will be a cure. Life expectancies have increased significantly during our time on the planet. Why should that ever stop?

We're not the first generation in quest of immortality, of course. Remember Ponce de Leon and his sixteenth-century expedition in search of the Fountain of Youth? We learned about him in school, because his search led, serendipitously, to the discovery of Florida. But Ponce de Leon was just one of thousands of seekers — from ancient Taoist philosophers and medieval alchemists to nineteenth-century purchasers of snake-oil from salesmen in the Wild West — who hoped to find the secret of eternal life.

But these folks were considered a little strange in their time. Now it's considered *normal* to spend thousands of dollars a year on cosmetic surgery, Botox treatments, anti-aging creams, and potions of all kinds. And that's just to *look* younger. Imagine what we would be prepared to spend to actually *be* younger.

Is it realistic to expect that we will be the generation that finally increases the human life span to its potential 120 years or so? Probably not. It is true that life expectancy at birth has increased an astounding 33 percent from the beginning of the twentieth century to the beginning of the twenty-first. But most thoughtful students of the longevity issue tell us that there won't be another increase like that any time soon.

Why not? Because a large part of that 33 percent was statistically due to decreased infant mortality. Advances in hygiene and sanitation, the development of antibiotics, universal immunization programs to control infectious diseases, and improvements in maternity care all combined to create the conditions in which most of us survive infancy and live to reproduce. In the early 1900s, the infant mortality rate in Canada stood at about 20 percent; now it's down to just over .5 percent. That improvement alone brings our average life expectancy way up. If you're reading this, you can thank medical science for the fact that you dodged the infant mortality bullet. But those early improvements in public health are doing very little for us now. They will make scarcely a dent in the odds of our surviving longer as we get older.

It's true that mortality rates from heart disease, cancer, and stroke, the three leading killers of women in Canada (and indeed all adults the world over) have shown comforting declines over the last twenty-five to thirty years, due to medical breakthroughs in treatment. And new discoveries are no doubt just on the horizon. But there just isn't room in the statistics for a continuation of the steady upward trend we saw over the last century.

And once we pass through our peak reproductive years, evolution isn't on our side any more. The process of natural selection has done a lot over the millennia to weed out the genetic defects that cause us to die young, for the simple reason that if we die before we reproduce, we can't pass on those defects. But natural selection does nothing at all to eliminate from the human gene pool those defective genes that don't show up until later in life. Genetic predispositions to adult-onset diseases such as multiple sclerosis, Huntington's chorea, and ALS (Lou Gehrig's disease) continue to be passed on from generation to generation. Genetic predispositions to diabetes, heart disease, and certain types of cancers show no signs of decreasing in populations. If anything, they are on the increase, as medical science enables adults with disabling diseases to reproduce later and later in life.

Aging also brings with it hormonal changes that affect the body's ability to function. For women the most dramatic of these changes is, of course, menopause (about which more later). These hormonal changes aren't life-threatening, although some of their symptoms — the fifteenth hot flash of the day by only ten o'clock in the morning — may feel like it. But they do pose additional challenges. For example, it's harder to keep excess weight off the abdomen after menopause than it was before.

And in addition to genetic diseases and hormonal change, there is the natural garden variety wear and tear on the body. Over the years,

WHAT ABOUT HRT?

Hormone Replacement Therapy has always been controversial. When the Women's Health Initiative brought its trial study of 16,000 women taking HRT to a premature halt in the summer of 2002, because the researchers concluded that the risks (specifically, an increased risk of breast cancer) to the participants outweighed the likely benefits, women taking HRT were understandably concerned, and fled HRT in droves. While it is now recognized that HRT is not a universal panacea for all the ills that beset women getting older — and most responsible doctors never thought it was — it still has a place in the treatment of the symptoms of menopause. Go to the New Women's College Hospital website, www.womenshealthmatters.com, and search Hormone Replacement Therapy. You'll find *A Guide to Hormone Replacement Therapy* containing a clear and comprehensive discussion of the issue.

simply as a by-product of the processes of living, we develop joint problems, thinning bones, weakened immune systems, and damage to our DNA. Our internal organs weaken and find it more difficult to perform their functions. Our muscles weaken and shrink unless we work hard to keep them strong and supple. Immune function declines somewhat, and we don't respond as well as we did in our younger days to antibiotics and other medications. We may experience a build-up over time of harmful substances, like "bad" cholesterol, blood fats, and blood sugars. The human body is, after all, just a sophisticated and amazingly intricate machine. And all machines break down eventually.

HEALTH ISSUES AND RETIREMENT PLANNING

These are matters we have to confront in the process of retirement planning. For some, health status was the factor that precipitated retirement in the first place, and you don't need to be told how important it will be to your future well-being. But even if you are retiring in perfect form, full of energy and vigor, you shouldn't take your good health for granted. You'll need it if you are going to realize your retirement dreams.

More than we may realize, health outcomes in retirement are within our control. We need to think about it now, while we've still got time to do something about it. We need to be realistic about our health, taking care of ourselves and taking any health problems — our own and our partner's — into account. If we don't, all of our other careful plans may come to naught.

Some useful women's health websites:

- **Women's Health Matters Network**
  www.womenshealthmatters.com
  Established by the New Women's College Hospital in Toronto. You'll find easy-to-use resources on particular diseases and conditions as they affect women, a searchable resource database on women's health and Le Club, a series of moderated, online discussion groups on a wide variety of women's health topics.

- **The Canadian Women's Health Network**
  www.cwhn.ca
  This organization puts out a magazine and a variety of research reports, all of which are available on the website. Check under "What's Hot" for news bulletins on the latest research on women's health issues. The website includes a searchable research database.

- **Chatelaine**
  www.chatelaine.com
  Go to this website and select "Health" from the Toolbar menu. You'll find useful and colorful articles, quizzes and online tools for managing weight control and healthy eating, downloadable, easy-to-use charts for tracking your daily food intake, and links to women's health related resources.

MENOPAUSE AND HORMONAL CHANGE

Before there were boomers, most women just shut up about menopause. It was one of those mysterious "female troubles" that everybody knew about, but nobody mentioned. Myths about menopause abounded. Whatever it might be doing to women, menopause made strong men tremble! They believed that menopause drove women insane (well maybe, but only temporarily!). They believed that it turned virtuous wives, mothers, and grandmothers into sexually insatiable viragos (they wish!). Certainly they believed, many of them, that it spelled the end of a woman's useful life on earth. No wonder the women themselves suffered in silence.

Suffering in silence is not, however, the boomer style. When we started to hit menopause in large numbers, it became NEWS! Menopause has spawned a rich recent literature. Much of that literature has an upbeat, countercultural flavor that focuses on the positives of menopause. Menopause is a time for regeneration, a new beginning, a new assertiveness. It's a time when we irrevocably say farewell to an important part of the self that has brought us this far, and embark on forging — or finding — the self that will take us the rest of the way.

These are certainly among the realities of menopause. But no amount of new-age gloss can camouflage the simple, stark fact that menopause isn't much fun. Going through menopause is an experience that most of us who have done it would choose not to repeat.

And no wonder. The symptoms that accompany menopause are legion. They include hot flashes, night sweats, vaginal dryness, urinary incontinence, muscle and joint pain, weight gain, accumulation of fat inside the abdominal wall, insomnia, thinning bones, mood swings, anxiety, depression, tiredness and lethargy, back pain, dry skin, loss of hair, thinning hair, loss of interest in sex, abdominal bloating, constipation, headaches, loss of skin tone, sagging and flattening breasts, breast pain, forgetfulness, loss of ability to concentrate, itchy skin, brittle nails, and dry eyes. The list is long, too long. If you're in the midst of menopause, you could no doubt expand upon it from personal experience.

There is considerable medical controversy over how many items on this list are hormone-related, and how many are simply the effects of what is regarded as "normal aging." Only hot flashes and vaginal changes are universally acknowledged to result from depletion of estrogen. But hormone-related or not, these symptoms came down upon us like the furies starting in perimenopause (the five- to ten-year period preceding menopause, in which hormone levels start to fluctuate and fall), and continuing throughout menopause.

Most of these symptoms will go away. We will not have to live for the rest of our lives with hot flashes (believe us, it's true). We will recover our ability to concentrate. We will sleep through the night again, once the transition is complete.

Other symptoms, however, are destined to become part of the permanent condition. A body that is not producing estrogen will not ovulate and menstruate. Estrogen is an important contributor to abundant, pigmented hair, bone density, strong, smooth nails, moist and supple skin texture. Estrogen depletion slows metabolism, contributing not only to increased fat retention, but also to redistribution of our body fat from hips and thighs to abdomen, where it will be much more damaging to our health. So post-menopause, we'll have to work harder at maintaining our bodies (for concrete suggestions on how to go about that, see Chapter 13). Not to stay competitive with the trophy wife, but to stay healthy. To stay alive. To *enjoy* our retirement!

THE CHRONIC DISEASES OF AGING

Here's a mini-glossary of some of the medical conditions we face as we age.

Cardiovascular Disease

Cardiovascular Disease (CD): A broad term referring to diseases of the cardiovascular system. This includes diseases of the heart and the blood vessels, including the blood flow to the brain. Cardiovascular disease is also referred to as circulatory disease.

Canadian Heart and Stroke Foundation website: www.heartandstroke.ca, Health Dictionary

We used to think of CD as a disease for men. It wasn't an issue for women, we were told. Odd, that, especially considering that CD is the number two (behind cancer) killer of women between the ages of forty-five and seventy-four, and moves into first place at age seventy-five. Exactly as it does for men. In fact, based on 1999 figures, the most current available, cardiovascular disease accounts for a higher percent of deaths among women than among men: 37 percent as compared to 35 percent.

Why did they tell us that we didn't have to worry about cardiovascular disease? Probably because CD appears to hit women at least ten years later than it hits men. Our hormones offer some protection until menopause. So while women are definitely at risk, they are not as much at risk for what the medical establishment views as "premature" cardio disease — the heart attack that kills the father of a young family or takes a productive worker out of the economy. The women who die of CD tend to be "old," i.e. retired, or never part of the workforce, with families that have left the nest. Not, perhaps, quite so visible a social problem, but just as lethal an individual problem for women who sicken and die because they didn't believe they were seriously at risk.

When the medical establishment began to notice that women *were* at risk for CD, a theory gained some currency that CD was a *new* thing for women. We heard that women began getting heart attacks when they adopted the "male lifestyle" and for the first time met up with — stress! Equality with a vengeance! Heart disease is the price women pay for their ticket into the world of work outside the home! But in fact, while the incidence of CD has certainly been on the increase over the last twenty years, it has increased for men as well as for women, largely as a result of gender-neutral lifestyle issues like smoking, poor diet, and lack of exercise. This should come as no big surprise to women, who always knew that the "female lifestyle" (you know the one we mean — the double day, the job without pay equity, the "feminine mystique") was loaded with stress.

Women do suffer from CD. But we were off the radar, and for years medical researchers didn't know or didn't tell us a very important — indeed potentially life-saving — fact. We now know that women with heart disease often present with very different symptoms than men. Remember those lists of the symptoms of heart attack we were bombarded with over the years? The strong, sharp chest pains, the searing pain running up and down the left arm? It turns out that these "classic" symptoms of heart attack often don't show up in women. For women, look for a different list of early warning signs of heart attack: heartburn, indigestion, weakness in the arms, nausea/vomiting, shortness of breath, feelings of anxiety, insomnia and other sleep disturbances, unusual tiredness, cold sweats, dizziness, and *maybe, just maybe,* pain in the chest, *maybe* extending up to the neck, jaws, and shoulder. Not so spectacular, but just as deadly!

We also now know that for women, the risk of heart disease increases dramatically after age fifty-five, and is related in large part to the impact of menopause. Check out the very useful website of the Canadian Heart and Stroke Foundation at www.heartandstroke.ca and use their online personal risk assessment tool to identify your own personal level of risk for heart disease.

> One of the roles of the female hormones is to protect the heart and blood vessels. Therefore, your risk of having a heart disease or stroke during or after menopause is four times greater than before menopause.
> Public Health Agency of Canada, Canadian Health Network, *FAQ About Women, What about women and heart disease?* www.canadian-health-network.ca

There are certainly risk factors for heart disease that are beyond our control. Family history, for example, is clearly something we can't change. Many of the most significant risk factors, however, are within our control. Exercise and a healthy diet have been shown in numerous studies to reduce the risk of developing heart disease for both men and women. Smoking enormously increases the risk of developing CD. If these and other risk factors make you a likely candidate for heart disease, be sure to read Chapter 13 for information on lifestyle changes that may save your life.

> Sex differences exist in cardiovascular disease hospitalization rates and procedures. Men have higher hospitalization rates than women for all cardiovascular diseases…All procedures are performed more often on men than women. Whether these differences reflect gender attitudes of health professionals or biology, or both, requires further study.
>
> Health Canada, *The Growing Burden of Heart Disease and Stroke in Canada, 2003*, p.vi.

Diabetes

Diabetes is dramatically on the increase in this country, to the point where it is now frequently referred to in the national media as an epidemic. While the disease is generally somewhat more prevalent among men than it is among women in Canada (15 percent of men have diabetes, compared to 12 percent of women), there is reason for concern. The most significant increase in diabetes rates in recent years has been among women aged forty-five to forty-nine. That's a 147 percent increase between 1978-79 and 2000-2001, as compared to a 125 percent increase for men of comparable ages. And for women the onset of diabetes, like heart disease, is correlated with reduced estrogen levels. In other words, for women, the risk of developing diabetes increases during and after menopause.

Type 1 Diabetes is an autoimmune disease in which the body fails to manufacture enough insulin. Formerly called juvenile diabetes, it tends to develop before age 30. It is not preventable, and is usually treated by daily insulin injections.

Type 2 Diabetes is a disease in which the body cannot effectively use the insulin it manufactures. It does not usually develop before age 40 (although in a troubling trend, it is now showing up as well among children and young adults).

The *Toronto Star*, Thursday November 3, 2005

What can we do to protect ourselves? Lots! In particular, we can get those damaging lifestyle habits under control. We need to maintain a healthy weight through diet and exercise, stop smoking, and limit alcohol consumption. Anybody who thinks she'd rather roll the dice on diabetes than abandon the comfort of her bad habits should visit the website of the Canadian Diabetes Association (www.diabetes.ca) and click on "What is Diabetes?" Then click on "Complications" and read carefully. It's not pretty. Many physicians say that Type 2 diabetes, the kind we develop when we get older, is almost 100 percent preventable among Canadians who are willing to adopt a healthier lifestyle. Enough said.

The Cancers of Aging

We don't yet know what causes cancer. But we do know that many common cancers are associated with aging. Scientists hypothesize a number of reasons for this. In their book, *Successful Aging*, Drs. John W. Rowe and Robert L. Kahn cite three factors for why we develop more cancers as we age:

- a build-up of "errors" in cells, leading to such cancers as prostate cancer, multiple myeloma, and chronic lymphocytic leukemia

- delayed effect of exposure or environmental carginogens (mesothelioma from exposure to asbestos)
- cumulative effect of exposure to environmental risk factors (skin cancer), carcinogens or lifestyle factors like smoking (lung cancer), and poor diet (colon cancer)

They do *not* cite the simple aging of cells. Old age does not cause cancer.

Gynaecological cancers can strike women at any age. Cervical cancers, for example, are more common in young women than in older women. Ovarian and uterine cancers, however, do tend to affect women after age fifty. Likewise breast cancer, the most common cancer to strike women, is most prevalent after age fifty. In fact, the risk of developing breast cancer doubles as we move from our forties to our fifties, and increases by another 50 percent as we move into our sixties. Overall, 1 in 8.9 Canadian women will develop breast cancer.

The risk factors for cancers are many and various, as are the preventive measures that can be taken to reduce the risk. Most experts agree that the probability of developing breast cancer is influenced by lifestyle. Again it's the big three: diet, exercise, and smoking status have all been shown to have a significant impact on the probability of developing breast cancer. Hormone replacement therapy has also been found to slightly increase the risk, though it also protects against hip fractures and colon cancer; the risk/benefit ratio should be carefully considered.

Check out the website of the Canadian Cancer Society: www.cancer.ca. At this easy to use website (which also links you to provincial Cancer Society sites), you can get detailed information about specific cancers, including treatment options. Click on "Prevention" for the latest research on the benefits of healthy eating, active living, and not smoking. If you enter "women" in the search engine, you will directed to a wealth of women-specific articles and resources, many of them on breast cancer.

Osteoporosis

Osteoporosis, a condition which results in a significant loss of bone mass, is yet another of the hazards lurking out there for women past menopause. Loss of bone mass is the cause of "dowager's hump," the bent spine that characterizes the stereotypical little old lady. Loss of bone mass also leads to bone fragility. Bones break easily and heal with difficulty. This can be much more than a debilitating nuisance — it can be fatal.

> A painful, crippling, and life-threatening condition, osteoporosis is the single most important health hazard for women past menopause — it is more common than heart disease, stroke, diabetes, or breast cancer.
>
> Dr. Miriam Stoppard, *Menopause*, Toronto: Random House, 1994, p. 66

Again, lack of estrogen is the culprit. Estrogen plays a significant role in facilitating calcium absorption, an important contributor to strong bones: when estrogen levels fall, women lose bone mass. It's that simple. Osteoporosis is not an inevitable accompaniment of the aging process, however. There *are* steps you can take to counteract the effects of reduced estrogen levels on your bones. (Lifestyle, lifestyle, lifestyle! See Chapter 13.) Regular weight-bearing exercise can arrest and reverse the process of losing bone mass. A diet rich in calcium, including calcium supplements and sufficient vitamin D to allow your body to absorb the calcium will help as well. Since smoking (both active and passive) also contributes to loss of bone mass, stop smoking now! There's no time like the present.

Alzheimer's Disease and Other Dementias

Newspaper headlines have described Canada as being in the grip of an Alzheimer's epidemic. Most Canadians, however, will age and die without ever experiencing dementia. Although cases have been diagnosed in patients as young as thirty, the statistical probability of developing the disease is relatively low prior to age eighty, and most Alzheimer's sufferers die of other causes before the disease reaches its terminal stages.

Dementia was formerly, and very misleadingly, called "senility," a term carrying with it the connotation that dementia was an inevitable accompaniment of old age. In fact, although age is certainly the most obvious and uncontroversial risk factor for developing Alzheimer's, scientists now believe that it is not caused simply by a deterioration in function of the aging brain. It is an identifiable disease, a pathology of the brain. At the moment, its causes are unknown.

The primary predictor of dementia is simply age, and there's nothing you can do about that. Nevertheless, there are now many studies demonstrating that "use it or lose it" applies to mental agility as much as physical. The mentally active certainly appear to be at somewhat lower risk for deterioration of brain function, including developing Alzheimer's. Brain exercises such as crossword and jigsaw puzzles, and math puzzles like Sudoku (really, we're not making this up to justify our own addictions!) have been shown to have a positive impact on cognitive functioning among the elderly. And some studies have suggested that physical exercise also improves brain function by increasing the flow of blood to the brain. So all that exercise you'll be doing for your heart and your bones may also have the beneficial side-effect of keeping you with it mentally!

Arthritis

Two-thirds of Canadians diagnosed with arthritis are women. Part of the explanation for this statistic is simply longevity. Arthritis is associated with aging, and women live longer than men. But even when age is accounted for, there is still a significantly higher incidence of arthritis among women than among men. Nobody is quite sure why this is the case, but it's a reality with which older women will have to contend.

Arthritis is more than one disease. It's a basket diagnosis for a bundle of diseases with quite different causes, symptom patterns, and outcomes. If you want to know all about it, go the website for the Arthritis Society, www.arthritis.ca, and read their lengthy list of different arthritic diseases, all with the common feature that a major symptom is musculo-skeletal pain. Our focus here is on the most prevalent form of arthritis associated with aging: osteoarthritis.

Osteoarthritis is often described as being caused by the normal aging of our joints. That's not strictly true — aging appears to play a part, but so does wear and tear. Most of us have abused or damaged our joints at some point in our lives by falling off our bicycles, carrying infants and groceries balanced on a thrust-out hip, skiing without proper conditioning, schlepping litigation bags to court. We've all done these, and worse. When the surface layer of cartilage covering bone ends breaks down, it causes the painful rubbing of bone on bone and reduced range of motion that characterizes osteoarthritis.

Is there anything we can do about it, once we've been diagnosed? Yes, of course there is. The joint damage can't be totally reversed, unfortunately. Cartilage is only given out once in a lifetime. When you've worn yours away, it's not going to grow back. But you can relieve the pain and restore restricted motion by getting those joints moving again. Weight control is important. If you lose weight, your joints won't have to work so hard to carry you around. And appropriate exercise is highly recommended. Consult your doctor, of course. You don't want to do further damage to joints that have already suffered. But you need to keep moving, or you may truly find yourself immobile.

Rheumatoid arthritis has nothing to do with wear and tear. It is an autoimmune disease. The body's immune system attacks the lining of the joints, causing inflammation, swelling, heat, and pain. It usually shows up between the ages of twenty-five and fifty. Rheumatoid arthritis can be treated and managed (although it cannot be cured) and serious joint damage can be prevented through proper medication. Symptoms of rheumatoid arthritis should not be ignored, since irreversible damage can be done if treatment is delayed. Like osteoarthritis, rheumatoid arthritis disproportionately affects women — three times as many women as men.

That Embarrassing Bladder Problem

It's a good bet that when you hit menopause, you made one change in your lifestyle — you've developed an intimate knowledge of the location of all of the washrooms in the places where you live, work, and play. For many women, menopause brings problems with bladder control. Again, blame loss of estrogen. Estrogen helps to keep the muscles that control the flow of urine from the bladder taut and flexible. When the estrogen supply declines, those muscles weaken, reducing their ability to control the flow of urine. This can result in leakage at unexpected and often decidedly awkward times.

However, help is at hand. Sometimes simple dietary changes will make a difference: not drinking less water, but pacing the timing of your water intake throughout the day, and limiting caffeine and alcohol. Reducing your intake of highly spiced foods, tomato-based foods, and artificial sweeteners can help.

Also very useful are Kegel exercises. If you ever bore children, you'll remember those. They were advised for post-partum women to tighten pelvic floors weakened by childbirth. They serve the same function for postmenopausal women in restoring muscle control over the bladder. How do they work?

Kegel exercises train the muscles of the urogenital tract controlling the flow of urine. To identify these muscles, the usual advice is to sit on the toilet and pee. Stop yourself in mid-flow, then let yourself pee again. Now, one more time. You've identified the muscles you need to work. Squeeze – release – squeeze – release. That's all there is to it. You can do this anywhere, and no one else will even notice. In bed, at your desk, in the car, watching TV. Just be sure to do ten to fifteen repetitions per session, holding for five to ten seconds per rep. Try for five sessions a day. You'll notice a difference very soon. Maybe you won't recover the bladder of a ten-year-old. But you won't have to plan your day's activities around the location of the washroom any more. And that's very liberating!

For more stubborn cases of chronic urinary incontinence, there is also medication and occasionally surgery. Consult your doctor. Don't let this problem drive you into social isolation. Life's too short!

Depression

Women in general are twice as likely as men to experience serious episodes of depression. On this front, however, there is some good news for women growing older; by the time women hit menopause, these sex differences begin to disappear, and by the age of sixty-five, women are no more likely than men to suffer from depression.

This does not mean that depression is not a problem for older women. The statistical improvement — 3.1 percent of women, down from 5.7 percent — still represents a lot of human misery. And certain life crises that come more frequently to women with aging, the death of a spouse, for example, may trigger depression even among those who have never suffered its debilitating effects before.

But don't accept it as inevitable! Depression is a treatable disease at all stages of life. If you're suffering, by all means get help.

Nicotine is commonly thought to have anti-depressant effects. But the truth is the reverse. People who smoked at least twice daily in 1994-95 had increased odds of having a major depressive episode as compared with non-smokers.

Canadian Institute for Health Information, *Women's Health Surveillance Report: A Multi-Dimensional Look at the Health of Women in Canada*, CPHI, 2003.

So all that sounds pretty depressing! What can I do about it? Read on! In the next chapter, we'll look at lifestyle changes that will help combat and counteract these health threats.

CHRONIC DISEASES OF AGING

Disease	Gender Issues	Lifestyle Factors
Heart Disease	• current data shows approximately equal death rates for men and women • men have higher hospitalization rates and more aggressive treatment	• smoking • diet • exercise • diabetes in women (diabetes is heavily influenced by lifestyle)
Stroke	• more than 1/3 of post-menopausal women have high blood pressure • no gender differences in death rates	• smoking
Osteoporosis	• affects 1 in 6 women, and 1 in 16 men over the age of 50 • particular hazard for post-menopausal women	• smoking • diet • exercise
Breast Cancer	• 1 in 8.9 Canadian women will get breast cancer	• diet
Arthritis	• arthritis affects 17.1% of women and 12.5% of men • women are more likely to be disabled by their arthritis • 55.6% of women over the age of 75 have arthritis	• diet • exercise
Diabetes	• more prevalent in men than in women in general • exception is aboriginal population, where women with diabetes outnumber men 2 to 1 • older women experiencing dramatic rate of increase	• diet • exercise
Alzheimer's and Other Dementias	• because women live longer, more women than men have dementia • 70-75% of dementia caregivers, both in the community and in institutions, are women	• exercise (positive impact for women only)
Obesity	• more men than women are obese • more women than men think they are obese • obesity is a particular issue for post-menopausal women	• diet • exercise

CHAPTER 13

Living Longer, Living Better

LIFESTYLE

"Entropy in the life table" is the scientific label for the fact that we will not see more major gains in life expectancy in our lifetime. But as individual boomers, we're not going to let entropy in the life table get us down. What we're really interested in is our own chances of beating the odds. We want to know what we can do, at this stage of our lives, to ensure a long and healthy life in our retirement.

The key determinants of longevity have been much studied, and are now reasonably well understood. Some of them, like heredity, were

Three of the most significant predictors of good health for Canadians are income, social status, and education. None of these things in themselves make you healthy, of course. These factors are simply proxies for the better health that often comes with more money — less stress because we feel more in control of our lives, informed access to better health care, and the ability to develop the personal skills required to maintain good health. In other words, they are proxies for the ability to practise intelligent self care.

always beyond our control. For others, like healthy childhood development, the horse left the barn long ago — it's too late to correct for any missteps we took in life prior to the age of six. But many of the health hazards lurking out there for older women are linked to something called "lifestyle." For health experts, "lifestyle" is shorthand for factors that are within our control. They're talking about all those bad habits you've developed over a lifetime that undermine your health: poor nutrition, lack of exercise, smoking, alcohol abuse.

It's never too late to substitute good health habits for bad ones. Sorry if we sound preachy, but it's true. We've all heard the messages. Get fit! Lose that spare tire! Forget the junk food! Stop smoking! We know — we've always known, really — that our bad habits could be killing us. But they're OUR habits and they're hard to break. They have seen us through the ups and downs of life for a long time, and it won't be easy to change them now.

But it's really not negotiable. After putting our health on the back burner while we got an education, held down a job, paid the bills, maybe raised a family, finally we need to make our own health a priority. This is a project that will take time. But now at last we have some time; it's "our" time, and there's no better way to spend it.

Interesting Canadian Statistics About Weight

- Canadian men in all age groups are more likely to be overweight than women
- At ages 20-29, **26.6%** of women and **40.7%** of men are overweight
- At ages 50-59, **53%** of women and **64.9%** of men are overweight
- Women with higher income levels are less likely to be overweight than women with lower income levels; with men, the reverse is true
- *Rich men are the most overweight group of Canadians:* **60.4%** of high income men are overweight, compared to **35.6%** of high income women

Health Canada, *The Growing Burden of Heart Disease and Stroke in Canada 2003*, pp.25-26

WEIGHT
The Obesity Epidemic

Body weight is an uncomfortable and controversial topic among feminists and boomers. Growing up and becoming women, we were bombarded relentlessly by images of waif-like female beauty. Remember Twiggy, and how we longed to look like her? The ideal of female beauty, as defined by those with the power to control the images, never did look like you or me. We fought those images, but we were seduced by them.

Now, after years of struggle, we've made peace with our bodies. We're okay with the fact that we're real women. We know that love, success, and happiness do not depend on reaching some arbitrary and unattainable degree of bodily perfection. We like ourselves so much better now. So why, oh why, can't we just forget about the whole weight thing? Like the billboard promises, "Fat can be fabulous!" Just leave us alone, please. Surely we've earned some respite from the relentless quest to lose weight.

Here's the problem. We're on the verge, here in North America, of what is now being called an obesity epidemic. Fat can be fabulous, but it can also kill you. And older women are very much at risk. It's not about how we look anymore. It's about how long and how well we will live.

Weight, Dieting, and Metabolism

Many of us have struggled with our weight for years, ever since adolescence, when that extra fifteen or twenty pounds arrived, courtesy of a wily Mother Nature who was setting us up for childbearing. We tried all kinds of fad diets. The grapefruit diet. The cabbage soup diet. Purging. Fit for Life. Atkins. The Zone. South Beach. Dr. Phil. We lost weight. And then we gained it again. And lost it again. And gained it again. Yo-yo dieting, it's called.

Why did we do it? We weren't really thinking about our health in those days. Mostly, we just wanted to be slim and sexy. Slim was successful.

And as we entered middle age, slim was youthful. So we continued our pursuit of the quick fix, losing the weight, gaining it back, and beating ourselves up for our lack of willpower.

We now know something very important that we didn't know then. All that yo-yo dieting is totally self-defeating. Embark on any extreme low calorie diet — and all those fancy diets, despite their promise of magic fat-burning ingredients and food combinations, are really just very low calorie diets when all is said and done — and initially you'll lose weight quickly. But soon that weight loss will slow down no matter how little you eat. And when the diet is over and you go back to normal eating again, you'll quickly gain all that weight back, and then some. Guaranteed! It's not because you ran out of will power. It's not because you're a bad person. It's because of what extreme low-calorie diets do to your metabolism. An iron law of physiology at work.

Here's what happens. Your body has more common sense than you do. It can't believe that you would deliberately starve yourself. If your body is deprived of sufficient nutrients, your body thinks that food must be scarce. To keep you from dying of starvation, it switches into hibernation mode, exactly like a bear going into a slow metabolic state to get through the winter. All your systems slow down. Your energy levels dip. Your metabolism becomes frugal, hanging on to every little bit of fat as long it possibly can.

Eventually, of course, if you stay at it long enough, you will lose weight, although it's a struggle. But a lot of that weight loss isn't loss of body fat; it's loss of muscle mass. So at the end of your diet, you may have met your weight goal, but you start the next phase one step forward and two steps back. Here's why.

First of all, your body's systems interpret the return of normal quantities of food as a signal to start frantically storing fat again, for insurance against the next period of scarcity. Provided with nutrients once more, your hormones kick in to instruct your body to store fat.

That's right, to store fat! And secondly, to compound the problem, your metabolism is still slowed down because you've lost muscle mass. Muscle mass boosts our metabolism; when our bodies are strong we burn calories faster. With less muscle mass, you have to reduce your calorie consumption just to stay in the same place. So unless you perpetually deprive yourself, all that fat you struggled and starved to get rid of is very soon back again, even if you're not eating to excess.

So you've yo-yoed a few times, and you're already in trouble. Suddenly, you're in your mid-forties. The pounds have crept up on you again. You're discouraged, of course, but you're not really worried, because you've always been able to get those excess pounds off with a few weeks back on Atkins or whatever your own pet fad diet is. So you go back on the regimen, expecting the same results you've always got. Bad news! This time, it doesn't work the way it used to. The magic bullet has lost its magic. What's going on?

We're getting older, that's what's going on. As we age, our metabolism slows down permanently. In *Fight Fat After Forty*, mandatory reading for any woman contemplating retirement who is sceptical about the need to pay careful attention to her diet and exercise regime, Dr. Pamela Peeke tells us that the metabolic slow-down rate is about 5 percent a decade after age twenty. At forty-five or fifty, our bodies burn about 15 percent fewer calories than they did when we were twenty, even without the effect of yo-yo dieting. If we continue to eat the same number of calories we

A woman who continually consumes 300 calories a day more than her body burns will gain weight at the staggering rate of thirty pounds a year. Let's assume that a woman requires 2,000 calories a day at age twenty to maintain her weight at her current activity level. That's a bit high for many of us, but it's close enough, and the math works. At age fifty, that woman will burn 15 percent = 300 calories less. So there you are — 30 pounds a year, without eating a single additional tub of ice cream!

Source of data: *Fight Fat After Forty*, Dr. Pamela Peeke

did when we were twenty, and maintain the same activity level, we will inevitably gain weight. Just to hold our own, we would need to reduce our calorie intake by 15 percent or increase our activity level to burn an additional 15 percent of calories. If we don't, there's trouble ahead.

This metabolic slowdown isn't directly related to menopause. It's simply the effect of aging. When menopause clicks in, however, weight gain can accelerate. The female hormones, estrogen and progesterone, promote the accumulation of body fat on the buttocks, hips, and thighs. As levels of these hormones decrease, testosterone, the male hormone that has always been present in women's bodies, begins to predominate and direct the storage of body fat onto the abdomen. And as you'll see in the next section, abdominal fat is bad news!

What's My Healthy Weight?

Before we talk in detail about maintaining your ideal weight, we need to forget about Twiggy and set some sensible targets. Most experts these days, including the World Health Organization, use the Body Mass Index (BMI) to determine healthy body weight. This index is based on weight/height ratios. BMIs between 18.5 and 25 are "healthy." Below 18.5, you're underweight. Above 25, you're overweight. Above 30 you're obese. A BMI above 25 is considered a risk factor for a number of the chronic diseases of aging, including:

- coronary heart disease
- stroke
- diabetes
- arthritis.

To determine your personal BMI, go to the website for Chatelaine, www.chatelaine.com, and click on "Health." The menu offers you a BMI Calculator.

There's really no magic number, of course. The BMI does not distinguish between men and women. Nor does it distinguish among body types. It does not award points based on whether your personal body mass is made up of muscle or fat. All of these factors will influence your personal healthy body weight. But calculating your BMI will give you a reasonable indication of whether of not you should be concerned about your weight. It's always a good idea to consult with your doctor.

Experts now believe that in addition to BMI, women should also be concerned about Waist to Hip Ratio (WHR). Not all fat is equally troublesome. For fat, just like real estate, location matters. Fat that accumulates around our hips and thighs — in other words, the fat of most pre-menopausal women — is unlikely to do us serious harm unless we are severely obese. But fat that accumulates around the abdomen is definitely a serious health hazard. WHR helps measure fat location. WHRs higher than .8 indicate the presence of a significant amount of abdominal fat, and require serious attention. Ratios less than .8 are more reassuring; they tell us that fat is accumulating away from the abdomen, and is less risky to our health. If menopause has converted your pear-shape into an apple-shape, a frequent occurrence, you have a higher WHR, and you need to be particularly wary of accumulating excess weight.

Both the Canadian Diabetes Society and the World Health Organization promote attention to the WHR. The Canadian Diabetes Society also counsels, however, that too much abdominal fat is hazardous

Examples:
Woman A: waist 30"; hips 40"; WHR = .75
Woman B: waist 30"; hips 35"; WHR = .857

If both women are the same height, Woman A will almost certainly have a higher BMI than Woman B. But Woman B, with less body fat overall, has accumulated more of her fat around the abdomen. She's at increased risk for coronary heart disease, stroke, diabetes, and arthritis.

regardless of WHR. If your waist measures more than 35 inches, you're at risk.

That Magic 10 Percent!

Maybe your BMI is 30, and you want to get down below BMI 25. At a healthy pace for weight loss, no more than one or two pounds a week, you're looking at months of dieting. On your bad days, you don't think you'll live long enough! Do not despair. Instead of aiming for what now looks like the moon, aim first for a more manageable goal: 10 percent of current body weight. Losing 10 percent of body weight and keeping if off has immediate benefits for your health. Your heart doesn't have to work so hard to pump blood through your body. Your bones and joints aren't under so much strain. Your insulin levels stabilize. You'll have a lot more energy. You'll live longer, so if you keep up the good work and go for another 10 percent, you'll get there eventually. And even if you don't get there, you'll have done your body a lot of good.

HEALTHY EATING

Healthy eating means not only how much we eat; it also means what we eat. This isn't a difficult point — a steady diet of tea and toast may keep the BMI below 25, but it will not provide the calories and other

More Interesting Canadian Statistics About Weight

- Obesity rates in Canada have more than **doubled** over the last 15 years for Canadians between the ages of 20 and 64
- Rates for women between the ages of 55 and 59 have **quadrupled**. **20%** of women in this age range are obese
- **14.2%** of Canadian woman are obese (2001 figures). The comparable rate for men is **16.7%**
- Obesity rates for women are highest in the their late 40s and 50s, with rates dropping slightly in their 60s

Andrew V. Wister, *Baby Boomer Health Dynamics: How Are We Aging?* Toronto: University of Toronto Press, 2005, pp.80-88 nutrients our bodies need to maintain bone and muscle mass, and fight disease and infection. We need to ensure that our daily food intake is high quality.

So it's back to the sensible approach and there's no better place to start than Canada's Food Guide. Take a look at the Food Guide on the Health Canada website (www.hc-sc.gc.ca). This Guide was significantly revised in 2007 and provides useful guidance for those of us trying to maintain a healthy weight. If you're trying to lose weight, though, the Food Guide prescribes too many calories. You'll have to adapt the amounts you consume, but you still need to ensure a balance — every day — of protein, dairy products, grains, and above all, vegetables and fruit. We cannot emphasize too strongly the health benefits of eating lots of vegetables and fruit. If you ensure a good variety, they will provide you with most of your daily vitamin and mineral requirements, as well as lots of healthy fiber, an essential for efficient digestion.

You also need to monitor your water consumption with more care as you age. You've been told for years that you should drink at least eight 8-ounce glasses of water a day to aid absorption and digestion of nutrients, flush waste products from the body, distribute oxygen, keep your skin supple, and lubricate your joints. We can't live without water. And it's even more important as you get older, since you dehydrate more quickly. You can substitute other liquids like herbal teas, mineral waters, and diet sodas (with the exception of colas), but never coffee or alcoholic beverages. Eight glasses is still the target, but if you drink caffeinated drinks and alcoholic beverages, you need to drink even more water because both of these beverages act as diuretics, flushing liquid rapidly out of your system instead of restoring it.

If healthy eating is going to require you to change the habits of a lifetime, you may need some help. Daily charting of what you eat and drink may seem over-programmatic at first, but it can be very helpful. You may want to check out the downloadable daily eating log on the

Tips For Healthy Eating:

- Don't skip breakfast, ever

- Keep healthy, tasty snacks on hand, so you can make good choices when you need something sweet or satisfying

- Get refined, processed sugars out of your life

- If you eat dense, complex carbohydrates, choose unprocessed versions, like brown rice, whole grain breads and pastas, which are good for breasts, heart, and bones, and may also discourage fat storage. Eat them early in the day

- Consider eating more foods containing phytoestrogens (soy products, chick peas, lentils, onions, apples, red wine), which may offer protection for breasts and bones as well

- Load up on fruits and vegetables

- Keep evening meals light and early

- Treat yourself from time to time — you deserve only the best! Don't waste calories on a box of cheap chocolates. Opt instead for one fantastic truffle

- Pay attention to portion size — restaurant portions, even if they're not super-sized, tend to be "man-sized"

- Get enough calcium, either through the consumption of dairy products (three servings a day for post-menopausal women) or through supplements, and make sure you get enough Vitamin D as well, to ensure good calcium absorption

- Some foods raise blood sugar levels and act as appetite boosters, while other foods act as appetite suppressants. Consumption of foods rich in refined sugars and processed carbs can promote binge eating, while foods rich in fiber, omega-e fatty acids, green tea, and other anti-oxidants may suppress appetite

- Keep fat consumption to a minimum, but make sure you get some fat. Eliminating fat altogether can result in hair loss, damage to skin tissue and other nasty surprises. Avoid saturated fats

Chatelaine website (www.chatelaine.com); much of the information you'll need to monitor healthy eating is printed right on their charts. When you go there, you'll notice that Chatelaine recommends women consume even more daily servings of fruit and vegetables than Canada's Food Guide advises: eight servings, as compared to the current Food Guide's seven for women over fifty-one.

EXERCISE
You need more!

We heard it, we knew it was true, and we felt guilty. Exercise = guilt. Because we never, never, never got enough. But surely one of the perks of aging is that we can stop fussing about exercise! Surely, as we get older, less physical activity will be exacted from us! Sorry, but it doesn't work that way. In fact, the opposite is true. Regular exercise is a critical ingredient in successful aging.

And not only do we need to exercise, we need to ensure that we get a full range of different kinds of exercise: aerobic training (endurance activities), flexibility training, and strength and balance training.

Boosting Metabolism
Here are some tips for kicking that metabolism back into gear and keeping it there. We can't personally vouch for the science behind all of these tips, but none of them are likely to cause harm:

- Exercise, especially weight-bearing exercise which builds muscle mass
- Eat dairy products — at least three servings a day
- Pay attention not just to what you eat, but also when you eat it
- Eat more lightly later in the day
- Eat breakfast
- Drink green tea

> Inactivity is as harmful to your health as smoking.

Health Canada, *Canada's Physical Activity Guide to Healthy Active Living for Older Adults*

How much exercise is enough exercise? Probably more than we think. Health Canada suggests that we should engage in flexibility activities daily, endurance (aerobic) activities four to seven days a week, and strength and balance activities two to four days a week, for a total of thirty to sixty minutes a day overall. Dr. Peeke, author of *Fight Fat After Forty*, has similar if slightly more specific counsel: a minimum of stretching (flexibility) every day, aerobic exercise for forty-five minutes a day, five or six days a week, and strength training sessions of thirty minutes' duration twice a week.

Both Dr. Peeke and Health Canada emphasize that to meet these targets, you don't need to set aside long stretches of time in the middle of a busy day. You can accumulate forty-five minutes of aerobic exercise by cobbling together a fifteen-minute walk to the post office, several trips up and down stairs from your home office at the top of the house to the laundry room in the basement, and an evening walk in the neighborhood to wind down at the end of the day. If you can't face that exercise bike, and the thought of joining a gym — again — fills you with loathing, don't worry. You can still meet your exercise goals.

Do something you really enjoy. Did you love to play volleyball or basketball when you were in your teens? Look for a women's league, and join it. If you can't find one, start one! Or dancing. Remember much you used to enjoy it? You never thought of it as exercise, but it can give you a cardiovascular workout to rival any aerobics class. Seek out dance classes. Or try Nia, a combination of aerobics, martial arts, and dance — it's all the rage now for women of a certain age.

There's an enormous range of activities that will help you get your daily exercise quotient. Here's Health Canada's list (and you'll be able to come up with ideas of your own) because you know what you love to do.

Examples of endurance (aerobic) activities
- Walking
- Swimming
- Dancing
- Skating
- Cross-country skiing
- Cycling
- Hiking

Examples of flexibility activities
- Stretching
- Dancing
- Gardening
- Washing and waxing the car
- Mopping the floor
- Yard work
- Vacuuming
- T'ai Chi
- Golf
- Yoga
- Bowling
- Curling

Examples of strength and balance activities
- Lifting weights
- Carrying the laundry
- Carrying groceries
- Climbing stairs
- Wall push-ups
- Weight-training classes
- Piling wood
- Standing up and sitting down several times in a row

Health Canada, *Canada's Physical Activity Guide to Healthy Active Living for Older Adults*

You already do lots of these things. Keep track of an ordinary day. It will give your morale a boost to realize how much of your daily exercise quotient is already in place. And forget "labor-saving devices" (remember them?). They were once touted as the path to women's liberation from household tasks. We've been trying all our lives to find easier, quicker ways to save steps and get things done. But we need to reflect on where all that labor-saving has got us in terms of physical fitness. If we walk briskly to the supermarket twice a week, instead of driving, we're well on our way to meeting our aerobic quotient for the week. If we carry those groceries home, we've knocked off at least half of our strength training. All without spending a nickel at the gym.

If you want or need to join a health club, choose carefully. Before joining, check with other users if at all possible, and ask questions. Some facilities have a reputation for offering vigorous workouts that are hard on the joints. You can't afford to risk that kind of damage. The International Council on Active Aging has put together a check-list for finding age-friendly health facilities, helping you rate accessibility, programs, and equipment. You can get a copy of this on the organization's website: www.icaa.cc.

SMOKING

If you are still smoking, stop. In 1997 the World Health Organization published a list of countries, comparing the numbers of heavy smokers they reported. Canada was seventy-first of the eighty-seven countries — for male smokers. But among women, Canada was seventh!

That is a truly frightening statistic. We've known for at least forty years now that smoking causes lung cancer and other respiratory problems. If we ever for a minute forget it, all we have to do is pull out a packet of cigarettes and look at the graphic and grisly photos that big tobacco is required to print on the side of the box. If you're reading this and still smoking, you've dodged the bullet so far, and you've probably got a few years left yet (45,000 of your fellow citizens a year in this country haven't been so lucky). You're deluged with anti-smoking public education campaigns, and there probably isn't a great deal more we can say to you that hasn't already been said.

But if a little more motivation will help, consider this. In addition to its contribution to lung cancer and other unpleasant, frequently terminal respiratory diseases, smoking is also a very significant risk factor in a number of the chronic diseases of aging. These include:

- coronary heart disease
- stroke
- breast cancer
- osteoporosis
- cervical cancer.

> Smoking is the principal, preventable cause of cardiovascular disease; it increases mortality by 50%, and doubles the incidence of cardiovascular disease.
>
> Andrew V. Wister, *Baby Boomer Health Dynamics: How Are We Aging?* Toronto: University of Toronto Press, 2005

Once a smoker stops smoking, the research shows that health benefits weigh in almost immediately; the damage of years can be virtually reversed in a few months. We don't often get such instant forgiveness for our sins. But if you wait too long to stop, your own personal stroke or heart attack or diagnosis of lung cancer could be just around the corner. So time is running out.

When you're ready, the Canadian Cancer Society offers an online support service at www.cancer.ca. Or you can call the Smoker's Helpline at 1-877-513-5333 for free counseling and advice. Many hospitals also offer free programs to help you quit.

> If you smoke a pack a day, you'll save $2,555 annually by quitting. If you put that money in your RRSP every year for the next twenty years, you'll have accumulated an extra $104,743!
>
> *Quit*, a 2007 publication of Smoke Free Ontario.

ALCOHOL

Excess alcohol consumption is a risk factor for a number of diseases at any age: many cancers (including breast cancer), cardiovascular disease, liver disease, and diminished brain function (loss of brain cells really happens — it's not just a party joke!). And there are a few issues older women especially should bear in mind.

When it comes to alcohol, men and women are not equal. Differences in body weight and body chemistry mean that alcohol causes impairment and long-term damage to women at lower consumption levels than for men. Health Canada classifies a woman who consumes more than nine drinks a week (a drink being a 12-ounce beer, or a 5-ounce glass of wine) as a heavy drinker. Men can consume fourteen drinks a week before they earn that dubious title.

As women age, their ability to consume alcohol safely is further reduced. As we now know, our metabolism slows down, and our bodies cannot break down and process alcohol as quickly as we used to. In addition, our body tissues lose water content as they age. As a consequence, alcohol in our bodies is less diluted, and we become impaired at lower levels of alcohol consumption. If your personal pre-menopause limit was two or three glasses of wine per party, chances are you're finding even that too much these days.

On the plus side, studies have now shown fairly conclusively that moderate consumption of alcohol, particularly wine and particularly red wine, has some positive benefits, offering some protection against heart disease and stroke to older women. This is the so-called "French paradox." So if you enjoy an occasional glass of wine, you can raise a glass to a reduced risk of cardiovascular disease. But only one glass!

> If health promotion programs reduce heavy drinking, and simultaneously encourage moderate drinking, the potential benefits to society could be enormous.
>
> Andrew V. Wister, *Baby Boomer Health Dynamics: How Are We Aging?* Toronto: University of Toronto Press, 2005

Family Relationships and Retirement

RETIREMENT: A NEW FAMILY DYNAMIC

When you visualize yourself in retirement, you may imagine you are as free as a bird, able to fly on your own at last, wherever the spirit takes you. If you're single, with no close family to include in your plans, you may really be able to live out this fantasy. If you've always made decisions for yourself, and lived with the consequences, you may have no need to consult with others about what you will do in retirement. You may decide by choice to factor other relationships into your retirement plans, but you don't have to; no one's needs or wishes will have anything like the same weight as your own. If this describes you, you can skip this chapter and head straight on to the next one.

For women in families, however, it's a different story. Like our less encumbered sisters, we may equate retirement with freedom. But for us, that "freedom fantasy" may be jarred back to earth very quickly by the competing fantasies of a spouse dreaming of a hot meal on the table at noon, or a daughter who needs a babysitter so she can go back to work herself, or elderly parents who need a personal care worker in their home. Other kinds of retirement dreams as well may be on a collision course with the needs and wishes of others — for example, our fantasy of spending more time in the bosom of family, finally compensating for too many hours squandered at the workplace, may clash with our adult child's desire to raise our grandchildren without any advice or interference from us.

Up to now, we've organized family life to accommodate our work schedules and work rhythms. We've achieved a balance, precarious and often unsatisfactory though it may be, between the demands of work and not-work. When we leave the workplace for good, that careful balance is upset in ways that many of us don't contemplate or plan for. When we went out to work every day, we developed very definite roles and identities in our family relationships — as spouse, sister, mother, daughter, daughter-in-law. Patterns and expectations became ingrained, almost second nature to us and our family members. But we're not working women any more. The ground has shifted. Some family members may want to keep these old relationships unchanged. But those old roles may not suit *us*. Especially if we have felt in any sense disempowered or victimized by these roles as defined by others, we will want and need to leave them behind to make new ones.

Negotiating new, post-retirement family relationships is an exercise that calls for lots of timely communication, and lots of flexibility. It's a challenge for everyone. But it's a particular challenge for women. There are still lots of societal and family pressures out there seeking to thrust us back into the old, stereotypical gender roles. Our families will be an important part of our retirement. But we may have some struggles ahead of us to make sure their expectations do not lay gender traps for us. It's an important part of the planning process to make sure that doesn't happen.

If you're hoping for a happy, meaningful, and productive retirement — and aren't we all? — now is a good time to remind yourself that some things are within your control and some are not. In crafting a relationships plan for retirement, we need to bear in mind that family relationships are very much a two-way street. If your retirement plans depend on other people, it's always best to check out *their* plans ahead of time, to make sure there's a fit.

COMMUNICATING WITH YOUR FAMILY

It's time for a reality check. It's time to get down, in stark black and white, our retirement fantasies, our plans and dreams, and to check them out, *really* check them out, with all our significant loved ones. Filling in the gaps will provide you with the opportunity for lots of dialogue with your family. Compare — realistically — the real and the imagined.

Here is an exercise you and your loved ones will benefit from. Do it first with your partner, then with other family members if they will be directly affected by your retirement plans. It will cover all the bases and lay the groundwork for frank and honest communication on this very important subject. Each participant must write down his or her list independently of the others (this is to avoid "copying" or spouse-pleasing or undue influence from any one). Then the comparison, and the conversation, can begin.

1. You:
   a. Write down your retirement fantasy.
   b. Write down what you believe is your partner's (or family member's) fantasy.
   c. Write down what you really think will happen in your retirement.

2. Your spouse:
   a. Write down your retirement fantasy.
   b. Write down what you think is your partner's (or family member's) fantasy.

c. Write down what you really think will happen in your retirement.

3. Sit down together and compare fantasies and realities.
   What matches?
   What doesn't?
   Repeat this processs with any other family members.

4. What will you do next? Listen! Communicate! Plan!

This sort of exercise, and the resulting discussions, can be eye-opening, and it can be downright brutal as well. You may have to revise your plans. So may your significant other. The essential thing is that you plan together, with communication and input from all family members concerned. And that includes you! Don't fall into old gender patterns. Don't become so accommodating that you forget to make room for your own wishes and aspirations.

Let's face it — if you have and live with a spouse, retirement is always a family decision. Almost all aspects of retirement planning will require that you both lay all your cards on the table. Retirement financial planning necessarily involves considering the income sources and expenses of the family unit. In theory, you can assess your retirement income on a basis completely separate from that of your spouse, just like it's possible to maintain separate bank accounts and separate credit cards. But it's not very efficient at this stage of your life. Retirement lifestyle decisions involve the two of you. Will you move to an apartment, or to Mexico? Will you cut your expenses, or will you start a small business to maintain your current lifestyle? Will you go back to school, or will you play golf every day? On some issues — golf's a good example — it's possible for you to go one way and your partner to go another. But on other issues, lack of consensus will defeat the whole project. Some of these issues probably have already had an airing at some time during your marriage. But in too many instances they have not been talked about. Mind reading is a very poor resource for planning.

In Chapter 1, we discussed the reality that men and women are not similarly situated when it comes to retirement. Statistically speaking, Canadian men are a couple of years older than their female partners, and they won't live as long. They are better off when it comes to retirement income. They have better pensions, and more money saved in RRSPs. In addition, women have had different career rhythms; male partners may be ready to retire on full pension just when their female partners are hitting their stride in a career they love and would be very reluctant to leave right now, or maybe ever. A husband who has "tolerated" a wife working full time may have very different and much more traditional gender expectations for retirement.

These issues and conflicting expectations may not be easy to resolve. If he wants to retire to grow vegetable marrows in small town Manitoba, and you're an urbanite with an allergy to compost, you've got a problem that will put a lot of pressure on the relationship. But you need to make sure that if issues like this arise, they will be resolved in a way that respects your autonomy and allows you to achieve your own retirement goals.

And if you follow our prescription for communication and planning, at least these issues won't come as a surprise just as hubby comes home from his retirement lunch!

YOU AND YOUR SPOUSE
A Good Companion: It's a Partnership

> *"You'll need a good companion*
> *For this part of the ride…"*
> — Bruce Springsteen, *"Land of Hope and Dreams"*

In a perfect world, our life partner is the person we have singled out from all others to share in every aspect of our lives. Our chosen mate is the person we trust with our most personal needs, feelings and desires, with our very lives. This is the relationship that makes you feel like *you*. This is the one person who probably knows you as well as you know yourself. In a really good spousal relationship, the burdens of daily life are shared and problems resolved. Quirks of personality and failings are recognized without damaging the relationship. Shifts are made to accommodate short-comings. Each is fully respected by the other. Both partners are encouraged and supported, critiqued and improved. Our sexuality is expressed and reciprocated. Each of us is nurtured. Rhythms are developed. As the marriage continues, age-and-stage modifications are successfully navigated. Pressures of work, childrearing, relocation, financial concerns, and career are negotiated. Successes are celebrated, failures acknowledged and accepted. A new life, a combined life, emerges and enhances both partners.

A successful spousal relationship also allows for the development of truly distinct individuals. We are not always just half of a couple. It's a partnership of two distinct personalities. Individual differences are encouraged and each can enjoy personal gifts and talents, hobbies, and pursuits that add to the fullness of the relationship.

But even in a good relationship, real differences may emerge as you plan for retirement. You have always been able to tell your spouse what you think and how you feel without fear of judgment, and can hear your spouse in the same way. Communication has not been a problem. But retirement discussions can raise entirely new issues. They can stir up some tough stuff. The casual banter of making decisions can now escalate into something more emotionally laden.

Communication: Negotiating Lifestyle Issues

So what will you do to make sure you stay on the same frequency? We've said it before, and we'll say it again: communicate, communicate, communicate! Negotiating retirement will have rough spots, but if you are not clear and firm about your position, how will your partner know what you truly want? He may think you are still undecided, still working things out. Maybe you need some practice in working out where to compromise and where to insist. Getting your needs met may mean doing some solo work in your marriage, making room for some separate activities. Maybe you have to be okay with traveling or playing bridge *without* your partner. But you check this out together. You need to keep talking to each other.

Communicating is a process. It requires skill and commitment. It takes practice. Real communication is a complex exercise in which each person actually hears the other person's position, his thoughts and feelings, and reflects them back again. Being judgmental has no place in real communication. Nor does refusing to acknowledge the thoughts and feelings of others. Real communication leads to a genuine exploration of issues, problem solving, and planning.

Let's set the scenario. Let's say you and your spouse need to talk about a serious and difficult issue. For example, you may want to retire before he's ready. You want to start volunteering, maybe do some traveling by yourself. You need to get this issue out on the table.

Try this exercise, with the co-operation of your spouse. Make sure he has fully bought into the value of the process and is not just going along with it to keep the peace! A generic framework for this discussion would look something like this:

- Spouse #1 introduces the difficult topic.

- Before responding, Spouse #2 must reflect back — fairly and accurately — what he heard: "What I heard you say was   . Did I get it right?"

- Both spouses must be in agreement about what has been said.

- Spouse #2 can then continue: "When I hear that, I think (this thought) and feel (this emotion)."

- Spouse #1 can then engage in the same way "What I heard you say was that you ▓▓▓▓▓▓▓ think and feel ▓▓▓▓▓▓▓."

Your discussion might sound something like this:

Wife: The school board says that I can retire at the end of June this year. That's official and I want to take it, even though you can't retire for two more years.

Husband: What I heard you say is that even though I can't leave the board for two years, you got confirmation that you can go the end of June and you want to go. Have I got that right?

Wife: That's right.

Husband: When I hear you say that, I wonder where you're coming from. I thought we were going together. I can't understand what made you think that you can retire without me. I feel confused and surprised.

Wife: So, I hear you saying, you thought we would retire together and my telling you I want to go in June surprises and confuses you.

Husband: Yes.

Wife: When I hear this I wonder where all the talking about my going to Nepal in September went. Now I am surprised and can't figure out what you thought about those plans. I feel you don't take me seriously.

Reflecting back and really understanding where your spouse is coming from is indispensable. Thoughts and feelings have to be sorted out. Now the communicating has begun, the draft of a plan is taking shape, and decisions will start flowing.

Who Will Do the Housework When You're Both Retired?

This is a big one. We've all encountered the prevailing folk myth of the retired husband who is always underfoot. He gets in the way as the wife tries to cope with the usual housework. She has her routines: Monday is wash day, Tuesday is vacuuming day, and Wednesday is bridge club. And now he's at loose ends, puttering around and making messes in the basement, wanting company, needing a hot lunch as well as meat, potatoes, and two veg for dinner. The core assumption of this dreary old folk myth, of course, is that "she" is a "housewife."

It's statistically improbable these days that you were a full-time housewife. But folklore dies hard, especially if it contains a grain of truth. And there's more than a grain of truth here. If you're like most Canadian boomer women, you have probably always done far more than your fair share of housework. Canadian surveys still tell us consistently that women do more domestic and family work than men. We did not win the battle over equal division of housework and responsibility for family maintenance. We let them get away with it. The best deal we got was "shared but unequal." Here's the question: are we prepared to accept the same deal in retirement?

> In 2001, 45% of women reported they did unpaid housework for 15 or more hours a week. Only 23.2% of men made the same claim. Almost twice as many men (13.3%) as women (7.5%) confessed to doing no unpaid housework at all.
>
> Statistics Canada, *Women and Men in Canada: A Statistical Glance*, 2003 Edition.

It could so easily happen. After all, if he didn't do his fair share while the two of you were working, his domestic skills are pretty rusty by now. Wouldn't it be easier just to do it yourself? Don't fall for it! Once you cease to go to work every day, at least on a full-time basis, domestic work and family maintenance will move in very quickly to fill the gap. The housework has to be done. There are meals to prepare, and laundry to do, and e-mails to send to the family about care for your elderly parents. Some of us may be wealthy enough in retirement to do what we always did — contract some of it out. But many of us won't. We can't eat out every night! And we didn't retire just to give ourselves more time to iron the sheets!

Don't postpone this housework discussion. Otherwise, before you know it, you'll be back to the same old patterns. You know how it works. Just like the frog in the slowly heating pot of water, we keep making small adjustments that don't seem big enough to complain about. Then we wake up one morning boiled. If your husband's first greeting of the day is "What's for dinner?" or he leaves every morning at dawn to play golf, you've got hard times ahead if you don't nip this in the bud right now. Of course you'll do your part — you always have. But now's the time to make sure he does too. This is not a rehearsal; you're not going to get too many more chances. So don't blow this one!

You'll probably have to set aside a dedicated time to discuss this. Almost certainly, your spouse is going to need a crash course in how to run a household. If you've been working outside the home yourself for the last thirty years, you may need a refresher course yourself. But you have to go into this believing that old dogs can learn new tricks.

Consider this approach.

- Make a list of essential domestic chores — the "house needs"
- Show the list to your spouse and ask for his version of necessary chores
- Label chores: "I can do" or "I have to learn to do"
- Rank chores: "I like to do" or " I don't like to do" (ideally, unless

by some miracle your likes and dislikes are a perfect match, each will get an equal number of both kinds)

- Divide up chores and designate who does them, how often and when; some will be his, some yours, and some outsourced
- Negotiate. Maybe you'd rather do something new, even if it takes some learning time, instead of a chore you're adept at, but hate
- Find and designate a regular convenient time to do chores. You don't want to be doing chores all the time!
- Try this for a month and re-evaluate.

Remember: he's not doing this for you. He's not "helping with the housework." You both live there. It's a joint responsibility. A "thank you" for every chore is not necessary and is not going to happen.

The Really Tough Stuff: Life and Death Decisions

Spouses take care of each other. There may be times in a marriage where one spouse must speak for the other when he or she cannot. Now that you're getting older, it's likely that serious health issues will have to be considered. There may be times when illness or incapacity will impair one spouse's ability to make decisions. For times like these, it is imperative that you know what your spouse wants and that he know your wishes. Knowing your spouse's most intimate thoughts and desires, and making sure that he knows yours, is the best insurance you can have that both your wishes will be respected and acted upon.

Do you know how your spouse feels about life supports and heroic measures after accidents, strokes, heart attacks, or surgery? Does he know how you feel about these things? These are tough conversations. Have you had them? Probably not. Let's see how you might go about it.

- It's a difficult subject. Admit it to yourself first.
- Approach discussing it with your spouse in a loving, caring

fashion. "I need to talk about something that is really hard for me, but is still important."

- Choose a convenient, private time that will be uninterrupted.
- Open with your own thoughts, feelings, and wishes.
- Confirm — you know how to do it now — that they have been accurately heard.
- Ask about your spouse's thoughts, feelings, and wishes.
- Feed back the information and make sure you both understand each other.
- Agree on a method to formalize both your wishes.
- Summarize and be sure you both understand.
- Be gentle with each other.
- Be alert to the possibility that this conversation will raise other issues that need attention.
- Return to this topic from time to time, have the conversation again, and discover whether or not things have changed for either of you.

This may sound grim. But in an emergency it will be invaluable, providing each of you with the permission and the strength to do what the other would wish.

Powers of Attorney

In a spousal relationship, partners normally step in for each other. But the law doesn't always see it that way. You can, and you should, make sure that your right to make personal, medical, and financial decisions for your spouse (and his for you) is formalized in a legal document that is usually referred to as a power of attorney.

Powers of attorney come in two general types. The first, a Power of Attorney for Property, gives you, the "attorney" or agent, the right to exercise legal control over someone else's property. If your spouse or your aging parent, for example, gives you a valid Power of Attorney for

Property, you can access their bank accounts, make arrangements to pay their bills, even sell their house if you want to. If you have exchanged Powers of Attorney for Property with your spouse, either of you can access funds from the other's resources to cover expenses. This could be very important in an emergency, particularly if one of you has managed the finances, and not everything has been kept in your joint names.

Conditions can be placed on a power of attorney: You can specify that it's only for access to certain bank accounts, for example, or provide that it ceases to have effect if you become incapacitated. Typically, however, powers of attorney are drawn up as continuing powers of attorney without any limitations. You wouldn't give someone your power of attorney unless you trusted them to use it responsibly and in your best interests, and these documents are often most needed when people can no longer manage their property for themselves. You should be aware, though, that a Power of Attorney for Property is effective as soon as it's signed. If you want to be certain it won't be used without your instructions, tuck it away in a safe place. Just make sure that someone responsible knows where to find it when it's needed.

A Power of Attorney for Personal Care (it may have a different name in your province — in Nova Scotia it's called a Health Care Directive, and in British Columbia a Representation Agreement) appoints your "attorney" as your agent to make decisions regarding your personal care, including health care. Unlike your Power of Attorney for Property, however, the Power of Attorney for Personal Care does not come into effect immediately. It only permits your attorney to make personal care decisions for you when you no longer have the capacity to make them for yourself.

Because these are powerful documents, the law requires that they be executed with some degree of formality. It is not necessary to go to a lawyer, although some people do that, often at the same time they are making a will. The forms that are required in your province will be available in legal stationery stores, in self-help kits, and often on government websites, usually with clear instructions on how to fill them out. Follow these instructions carefully.

Contrary to popular belief, a Power of Attorney for Personal Care is *not* the same thing as a "living will." A "living will" or "advance health care directive" is a document recording your instructions for what to do in certain health crises — for example, your wish that in the event of brain death, you do not want to be kept alive on a respirator. In some provinces, no particular formality is required for a living will; in others, these too are governed by legislation. If you want your "attorney" to be bound by your wishes, you should attach your "living will" to the Power of Attorney for Personal Care. If you've truly communicated with your spouse on these issues, sharing your most intimate wishes, your spouse will already know what you want and vice versa, and you'll both feel better for having talked about it before any document is drawn up.

Spouses usually act for each other as attorneys for both personal care and property, but other family members or professionals may be named in addition or as alternates. Consideration, care, and communication are necessary before drawing up these important documents. The attorney should be kept informed, particularly with respect to personal care, as these wishes often evolve and change.

Ontario's Ministry of the Attorney General offers a free Powers of Attorney kit, including all the necessary forms and information. This kit can be downloaded from the Ministry's website at www.attorney-general.jus.gov.on.ca (you'll find "Power of Attorney" on the sidebar menu) or ordered from the Ministry. Also on the website is a very useful Q & A booklet that answers questions in clear, non-legal language. The kit and information conform to the laws of Ontario. If you live in another province, don't use them without checking to make sure they'll be valid where you live.

The Role of Spousal Caregiver

Adult female relatives do the greatest amount of intimate caregiving in our society. Mothers, wives, sisters, daughters-in-law step up to take care of the men — and each other. Woman may retire earlier than they expected, giving up careers when called on to be home because of a husband's ill health or disability. If women caregivers are not careful, they may end up isolated in their homes, chained to their partners with the bonds of love and duty, confined to a role they may be very ill-adapted to perform.

However much we love our spouses, however devoted we are to their welfare, women who must care for a dependent or disabled spouse may become frustrated and resentful. Our menfolk are rarely at their best with immobilizing disabilities. A disabled spouse will certainly be feeling that his privacy and autonomy are threatened. We may soon begin to feel that ours is as well. As our spouse's world shrinks and we become increasingly the center of his universe, we may begin to feel under surveillance, constantly monitored and judged as we go about our daily activities. We may lose patience when our every move is questioned or commented on — our private phone conversations overheard, our tête-à-têtes with friends suddenly joined by an extra participant, our trips to the supermarket timed. The caretaking spouse must take on the roles of co-ordinator, manager, and facilitator. She calls the doctor, supervises the medication, arranges visits to the optometrist and the chiropractor. She may soon find she's taking on other roles as well: the role of mother, the role of nurse.

It's not healthy. You're not his mother. You're not his nurse. You're his partner, and you're not doing him any favors if you don't fight for your own life and your own dignity. Don't try to be superwoman. This isn't a loyalty test. You might get by on grit and determination for short-term illnesses, but for long-term and chronic care — cardiac rehab, paralysis, dementia — more planning and discussion is required. You may need to bring in reinforcements. Issues of expectations and capabilities have to be addressed. Honesty, frankness, and communication can be invaluable supplements to love and devotion, heading off resentments and feelings of entrapment on one side, and feelings of betrayal and abandonment on the other.

Just remember, if you are the one to require care, it's very likely that your spouse would find a better, more practical way to care for you than giving up his life and activities. Take a page from his book, and make sure you do the same.

Death of a Spouse

One of the greatest losses we will sustain in our lives is the death of a beloved spouse. The loss of a spouse is like the loss of a significant part of ourselves. It will bring with it the loss of emotional, social, and financial support, but more fundamentally, it will challenge the way we define ourselves and our world. Perhaps over the years you put all your eggs in one basket, focused on your spouse, and placed a decreasing importance on other relationships. Now you must deal with your emotional reaction to the death, and at the same time with a profound disruption in role, routines, and relationships with others. You may lose identity and status in the community. Marriage is a social unit, and it often defines a woman's place in the world. The death of a spouse forces a woman, at a time of bereavement and vulnerability, to seek out her own identity, and her own supports and resources. She will have to learn new skills and carve out her own place in the community. She may have great difficulty dealing with being alone.

Sadly, it's important that we prepare ourselves for this possibility. The reality is that more women than men survive to an advanced age, that women are typically younger than their spouses and have a significant probability of outliving them. It's also true that men are more likely than women to remarry in later life. There's no doubt that women are more likely to be alone as they get older. With this in mind, we should "widow-proof" ourselves as best we can. We need to fully understand our family's financial situation. We need to make decisions about our lifestyle and how we will spend our time. We must develop and nurture relationships that validate and support our individual identity.

The loss of a spouse is devastating, but most of us do survive it, and adjust to our new status. Some women even find a new energy in being independent and self-reliant. Self-help groups are often effective in easing the adjustment to widowhood. When time has alleviated their grief at the death of a beloved spouse, women often report a new sense of competence and freedom. There are many useful websites that can help us through the grieving process. Take a look at www.griefhealing.com.

Canadian Facts About Women Alone

- **38.3%** of women 65 and over live alone, compared to **16.8%** of men.

- In 1968, the divorce rate was **54.8 per 100,000** population. By 2003, it had more than quadrupled, rising to **223.7 divorces per 100,000** population

- **75%** of divorced men remarry, compared to **65%** of divorced women

- The probability of remarriage for women between the ages of 35-50 is **48%**, compared to **61%** for men, and continues to go down with age

- At every age and stage, more women than men live alone in Canada

Sources: *Women in Canada*, 5th Edition, Statistics Canada, 2006 and *Divorce: Facts, Figures and Consequences*, prepared by Dr. Anne-Marie Ambert, York University, for the Vanier Institute of the Family, 1998.

Marriage Breakdown

The fact that women are likely to outlive their spouses is part of the explanation for the disproportionate number of older women who live alone without partners. But it's not the only contributing factor. High divorce rates also mean women are left on their own. And a surprising number of those divorces take place after couples, many of them long married, have retired.

What if your spousal relationship doesn't survive the transition to retirement? There's no doubt that relationships, even those of very long standing, can come unglued in retirement. Like a host of other issues we've talked about in this book, issues of intimate personal relationships have often been put on the back burner by working couples. Infidelities can be papered over rather than dealt with, when you're both stressed out from work and there seems to be no time for counseling. Different priorities about money can be ignored when you're both still earning and there seems to be enough money for everything. Even serious incompatibilities — fundamental value issues — can be left unexamined when you're raising a family and preoccupied with your jobs.

But now you're facing retirement. And you decide, suddenly or maybe not so suddenly — maybe you've been contemplating this for a long time — that the man you're with is not somebody you want by your side for the duration. Before you act, stop and think:

- Know why you are ending the marriage
- Get professional counseling or therapy if you need it
- Do a hard-headed cost-benefit analysis — maybe he's not perfect, but if you dump him, you're statistically likely to end up alone. Are you ready for that?
- Make a concrete plan, including finances and a place to live
- Verify that your plan is watertight — consult with professional advisors
- Get legal advice.

If you're sure you know what you're doing, go for it! It's your life, and you've got a right to decide that enough's enough.

And what if he beats you to the punch? What if he dumps you before you can dump him? You've slogged it out making compromises against your own interest, financed his education, and kept his bed warm. You deluded yourself that the couples' therapy had worked, and now he says he's had it and he's out the door. This may be a tougher scenario for you to cope with — instead of friendly, or at least civil, termination negotiations, you're on your own. Use this as an opportunity to make sure you get what you deserve and need now from the divorce, even if you never had it before. Find yourself the best, most experienced lawyer you can afford, connect with a good therapist, and stop doing his emotional work for him. Take the time you need and start again.

Getting the best for you, of course, doesn't have to mean destroying him. Good divorces are better than bad marriages!

YOU AND YOUR CHILDREN: ALWAYS A PARENT

Some of us contemplating retirement have fledglings still in the nest. Because we were older when we had our children, they may be still in high school, college, or university. They still need our money to pay their tuition. They come "home" for the holidays, and depend on free room and board to stretch their summer earnings. They may never be there at mealtime, but they still expect groceries in the fridge and a never-depleted supply of laundry detergent and toilet paper. We understand that dependent children are part of our reality, and we'll have to take them into account in our retirement planning, at least for a while.

For others, your children are grown. You may be saying to yourself, "Been there, done that!" Why are we still talking about the children? They absorbed the lion's share of our time, energy, and money in our "middle" years. But that's over. Our kids made it to adulthood — with lots of help from us — but now they can fly on their own. This is "our time," after all.

Regardless, the truth is that the child-parent relationship doesn't go away. It evolves, bringing with it new joys and sorrows. Even after our children become adults, we may still find, if we're not careful, that parenting entails burdens and responsibilities that fetter our efforts to realize our retirement hopes and dreams.

We love our children. We wish them only the best. But now that we're planning for retirement, it's time to negotiate a new relationship, setting aside as much of the emotional baggage of parenting as we can. Consider the most common sources of potential conflict between parents and their adult children:

- Issues about on-going living arrangements
- Issues about child care
- Issues about money and inheritance.

Conflict and misunderstandings about these issues between you and your children can have a profound impact on your retirement plans.

We have earlier talked about the importance of clear communication and planning in negotiating your relationship with your spouse. So it should come as no surprise to discover that we give you the same prescription for dealing with your children. The key to successfully negotiating the shoals of the parent-child relationship in retirement is — once again — really communicating. As with any other negotiation, it is essential that we truly hear the other side of an issue. Communicating one's needs without recognizing and understanding what the needs are on the other side is a control tactic, not a problem-solving strategy. Don't do it — and don't let others get away with it, not even your well-loved children.

CLIPBs and Boomerang Kids

In the folklore of the 1970s, a mother dreaded the day when the nest was empty. Her occupation gone, the suburban housewife rattled around an empty house, took up drinking or bridge or therapy. The retirement of her husband a few years later at least gave the poor woman some company.

Now, it appears, the empty nest may be a thing of the past. The nestlings stay and stay, and even if they leave for a while, they come back. Perhaps they have graduated from university, and are having trouble finding a job. Perhaps they are saving for a car or a down payment on a condo. Perhaps a relationship has broken down and they need a temporary haven. Sometimes when they move back home, they bring partners. Sometimes they bring children, your grandchildren. The phenomenon is common enough to have a name: Children Living in Parents' Basements (CLIPBs) or Boomerang Kids!

> [A]n adult child returning home has become a fairly common, predictable event in family life.
>
> Statistics Canada, "Junior Comes Back Home: Trends and Predictors of Returning to the Parental Home", Pascale Beaupre, Pierre Turcot, and Anne Milan, *Canadian Social Trends*, 2006

Maybe you read about this phenomenon in the newspapers. Or maybe your twenty-four-year-old daughter told you all about it as she moved your sewing table out of her old bedroom, and unpacked her suitcase. "Everybody's moving back in with their parents now, Mum," she calls out breezily as she walks out the front door. "And please lay my black jersey dress out *flat* after you wash it. It can't go into the dryer!"

It's up to you how you respond to sharing a house with your adult children. Maybe you don't think it will interfere with your life in the slightest. Maybe you even welcome it. But chances are your children's new plans are going to cramp your style. You've got to address the issue, head on and early. A good confidence builder for putting your cards on the table is the firm conviction that having raised your children to adulthood and given them the tools for self-sufficiency, you've done your job as a parent. If your child doesn't use those tools, that's not your responsibility. We can't say it's not your concern. Of course you'll be concerned if your children are having trouble. But it's not your responsibility. Don't let guilt drive your decision-making.

If your grown son wants to move back home, and you've got the space in the basement and the stamina, consider taking these steps:

- Negotiate and collect a reasonable rent
- Ask for a reasonable contribution towards communal food supplies and household items
- Insist that communal spaces be kept clean and neat and that these areas not be taken over as his personal recreational space
- Do not provide maid service. Insist that your son take care of personal maintenance, including laundering his clothing and linens and keeping his room clean
- Establish a schedule of shared household chores, like taking out the garbage, loading and unloading the dishwasher, shoveling the snow, planning and preparing meals, doing grocery shopping
- Insist on basic inter-adult courtesies, like keeping the noise level down, keeping you reasonably informed of his whereabouts and whether he intends to be home for meals
- Enforce respect for the house rules. A "no smoking" rule applies to everybody. If you're recycling to save the environment, or turning the lights out and the heat down to save on electricity, he has to participate too
- If companions are a problem, make it clear that you will provide shelter for him, but not for his friends.

It's your house. You're the landlord. Whether you share it, and on what terms, is your decision.

If your daughter's move home conflicts seriously with your own retirement plans, if you need to downsize or turn your spare bedroom into a home office, you may have to take more drastic measures. Talk it through with her. Make it clear that she must have a practical, workable plan for finding a job, or there's no deal. You should agree on a timetable for her to find her own accommodation. And you should stick to it, even if she doesn't do her part. You raised her with survival skills. She won't starve on the street for long.

Does Grandma = Babysitter?

Are you ready to be a grandmother? This life experience, too, usually comes packaged with adult children. Grandparenting brings with it much joy and satisfaction. But it also brings with it some 1970s stereotypes that interfere with retirement planning — in particular, the notion that grandmother, now that she isn't "working" anymore, will take her greatest pleasure in babysitting the grandchildren. And she's always available!

In some cultures, a healthy grandmother is a logical and preferable alternative to daycare, enabling a working couple to leave their children guilt-free (and usually cost-free into the bargain) with a loving family member while they work to pay off the mortgage. If that role attracts you, fine. But if it doesn't, it's important that you communicate this message early to your children, in order to allow everyone to make their plans based on reality, not fantasy. And don't let anyone guilt you. Assure your children that you will always be there in a true emergency, but you've earned your retirement, and you intend to enjoy it. It's not your job to parent your children's children. That's their job.

Money: Communication about Expectations

What do you owe your children in terms of ongoing financial support, and for how long? If you could afford it, you probably helped pay for their undergraduate education and were happy to do it. But what if your children decide to go on to graduate school, or law school, or medical school? Post-doctoral studies? Internships in film and theater? Do you have to stay in the saddle until they can make it on their own, no matter how long it takes, and by what circuitous route?

For this one there's a simple answer. Of course not! If you would like to help out financially, and are in a position to do so, make it clear that it's a matter for negotiation, not a done deal. If you don't want to — or can't — don't worry about it. Just say no. Many successful doctors have worked their way through medical school, and your children can too.

And what about an inheritance? We have already discussed how to marshal your assets to pay for the retirement you want. For most Canadians, the family home and RRSP savings are your largest assets by a fairly wide margin. If you plan to convert them to retirement income — and most of us will, sooner or later — there may be little or nothing left for the next generation. Is that a problem you should be concerned about?

Once again, if you have raised your children to adulthood and given them the tools for self-sufficiency, you've done your job as a parent. You earned your money, and you don't owe it to your kids! But in order to avoid misunderstandings, make sure your children are at least generally aware of your plans. Your will is your own business, of course, but you don't want your children out there, in nineteenth-century fashion, incurring debts based on "expectations," if their expectations will be in vain.

You don't *owe* them. But maybe leaving some assets behind is important to you. Maybe there's a special family asset — a summer cottage, for example — that you want to preserve intact for the next generation. Or maybe you've got a child with disabilities, and are worried about his future when you're not here to provide. If that is your concern, there are lots of books out there on estate planning, and a good financial planner will have some ideas (insurance products or special purpose trusts tailored to your needs, for example) that can help you maximize the likelihood that you'll have something left over in your estate. The sooner you start planning for this, the more likely it is that you will be able to achieve your goals.

If you've got a little extra cash, of course, there's probably nobody you'd rather share it with than your children. Don't overlook the possibility that it will be more use to them now — when they're trying to buy houses and raise families — than it will be thirty years from now when you're dead and they've found their feet financially. Talk to them about it using the communication techniques we've outlined in this chapter. It will pay dividends in the end, in more ways than you think.

YOU AND YOUR PARENTS: THE SANDWICH GENERATION

If you have not yet figured out what "sandwiched" means, you soon will. You are the filling, the meat in the sandwich. One piece of bread is your parents (or other dependent elderly relatives) and the other is your children. It would be pushing the metaphor to say you'll be eaten alive, but you may feel like it at times. Overwhelmed, defeated, overextended. You have to say no to your daughter when she asks you to babysit your grandchild, because you have to drive your father to his dental appointment. You can't go on vacation — and you couldn't afford it anyway — because you're renovating the basement so your son can move back home. Just when it looks like you finally have some time set aside for your spouse, your parents' failing health requires your presence. And not just failing health. There may be safety issues, financial concerns, transportation needs, house repairs and maintenance, meal planning, shopping, and on and on. You feel victimized by siblings who live on the other side of the continent (or maybe only in the next city!) and simply assume that you'll do whatever caregiving is required. You feel as though you have no time to yourself. You wonder why it's always up to *you* to take care of everything and everybody.

It's hard to step away from caregiving. Women are conditioned to help, to be selfless in the face of others' needs, to try always to make things better. But remember the last time you were on an airplane? You were told that if the aircraft encounters trouble and the oxygen mask descends, you put *your* mask on first, before offering aid to others, because if you're not safe and healthy, you can perish in your struggle to help others. This message applies to life, as well as to airplanes. You must take care of yourself, and set boundaries. It is not reneging on your responsibility to find others who can stand in for you when family members need help. You don't need to do it all yourself if someone else just as suitable is available. Find a cleaning service or meal delivery service for your parents, a tutor or coach for your child's homework. Get some help in your own home. We're actually not indispensable. Maybe it will take more negotiating with your partner, or more delegation. But give up on doing it all yourself. You can't, and you shouldn't try.

A useful resource for those with care-giving responsibilities is www.familycargiversonline.com.

Negotiating Issues of Aging with Our Parents

Why are your elderly parents still rattling around in their big house? Why are they piling up utility bills, struggling with the yard work and paying higher and higher taxes on a property that is so much bigger than they need? Why do they still keep your brother's room ready for him? After all he is married, has small children, and lives 3,000 kilometers away!

Canada's 2002 General Social Survey reported that about **2.6 million Canadians between 45-64 still had children under 25 living with them at home.** About 27% of these people also performed elder care duties. Canadian women spend significantly more time than men do on both child care and intimate elder care.

Statistics Canada *Perspective*, Cara Williams, "The Sandwich Generation," September 2004

Why do they still keep a car, when it's mostly parked in the garage? Why do they still have to drive across town to their doctor? Why are they still complaining about their reading glasses and not taking steps to see the optometrist? Why are they wearing the same old clothes every time you see them? Why don't they go out to the programs at the community center? Are they keeping up with the shopping? Who's doing the cooking? Are they eating well? Have they updated their wills? Have they got a living will? Do they or don't they have powers of attorney for health care and finances? What happened at their last visit to the doctor? Why is your father suddenly using a cane?

There's only one way to find out. Communicate, communicate, communicate! Sit down and talk about it. Put your cards on the table. Use the communication techniques we've already used so effectively with our spouses and our children. Let's acknowledge the difficulties. With parents, there's may be lots of baggage — issues of privacy, guilt, shame, and fear as we delve into deeply personal issues of finances, health and hygiene, and funeral arrangements. In initiating these conversations, do not underestimate your parents' need to protect you from their problems and appear competent. Remember change is very difficult and they may fear disruption. Sit down and listen. Do this respectfully. Do it a lot, before moving to the solution stage or offering unsolicited advice. Once you get to the problem-solving stage, leave lots of room for your parents to take an active part in determining solutions.

It may be difficult, but it has to be done. So do it.

Housing

In Chapter 7, we talked about planning for your own retirement housing. If you're finding that your own house is getting to be a bit much to look after, and you're considering downsizing, you can be sure that the same issues are plaguing your parents, especially if they're still in the family home. Perhaps your parents are no longer able to look after themselves.

Most moves for the elderly are overdue, and often happen because of a crisis: a fall or the complications of an illness.

Should your parents move in with you? That's a question that only you, your spouse and your parents can answer. It may be a workable solution for your family. But don't overlook the difficulties. It is amazing how competent women become children in their mothers' presence, reliving old patterns of behavior. If you are used to running your own life and your own household, and so is your eighty-five-year-old mother, it may do damage to both your sense of autonomy *and* hers to try to set up housekeeping together. Consider the options for retirement living we discussed in Chapter 7. With so many options to choose from, you'll find something that works for both you and your parents.

When the time comes for a move, bear in mind that moving house is very stressful. The very practical issues involved may seem totally beyond the capacity of elderly parents, confused by too many details and lack of experience. If it's time for a move, don't back off. Their lives may depend on it. But be gentle. It's important that questions of moving be dealt with in a non-threatening way, or family bonds can be damaged at a time when you're all very vulnerable and need them most.

Our Parents, Ourselves

Our parents are concrete, visible exemplars of the aging process. We see the vital, active mother and father of our childhood turn into fragile, forgetful, dependent "old people" right before our eyes. We may see them struggle with technology and automation. We may see them become timid in the face of bureaucracy and authority figures. We see them succumb to the diseases of aging: arthritis, osteoporosis, cancer. We see them suffer from chronic diseases that have devastating effects on their bodies. It's painful — for them and for us.

If we're honest with ourselves, we'll admit that part of our pain comes from the fact that when we look at our elderly parents, we're holding a mirror up to ourselves. But let's learn from our parents, as we have always done. We can't stave off aging. But we can ward off some of its worst side-effects. If our parents have gotten themselves into difficulties in old age because they procrastinated about the tough issues, let's make sure we don't do the same thing ourselves. Our parents' old age has probably highlighted for us the importance of having a plan in place for aging and mortality. Now that we know this, let's make sure we make one for ourselves!

Dealing with Bereavement

Our parents do die. Death doesn't end the relationship, but it certainly ends a great deal. We are left with our memories. We'll replay, remember, and relive the relationship over and over in our heads. We will have regrets. Regardless of what we have done, we'll wish we had done more. If the relationship was on solid ground, we will mourn the death of a dearly loved person. If the relationship was difficult, the bereavement will be difficult, and likely even more painful — we thought we still had time to straighten things out and fix the hurt, but time ran out on us. And we will still mourn.

No matter how old we are, while our parents are still alive we feel we have a backstop, a safety net. We feel there is someone there, older and wiser, to guide and protect us, even if their real ability to do so has long departed. Intellectually we know that our parents are old, and the natural order of things is that they will die before us. And when they do leave us, we know that grief is normal, and the worst will pass. That knowledge doesn't avoid the pain and sorrow, but it does help us go on.

The last act of our relationship with our parents may well involve planning and attending their funerals. Communicating with them throughout their lives, and especially about this eventuality, will ensure that we can participate in this ritual as a loving child. As they did for their parents, and as we hope our children will do for us.

CHAPTER 15

Non-Family Relationships in Retirement

WHY ISN'T FAMILY ENOUGH?

As social animals, we thrive in relationships. Our family relationships have challenged us and given us strength and nurturance throughout our lives, and they will continue to do so as we contemplate retirement. If we've been lucky in our families, it's likely that family will be at the core of our relationships in retirement. Couples who are both retired may be fortunate enough to find much of the community connectedness they need in each other.

But we're not all so lucky. There are some very practical reasons why women retiring in the twenty-first century should attend to the nurturing of relationships outside of families. While some of this is obvious, it needs to be said. For increasing numbers of women, the nineteenth-century image of cozy family life is a faint and distant memory. It's not that kind of world any more, if it ever was. Many women reach retirement without partners. Many women never had children. Many women have lost their parents by the time they reach retirement age. Some are estranged from their families. Increasingly, we may live geographically distant from extended family members, if we have them. The result is that many women simply cannot look to family to meet their social needs. For these women, their non-family friendships and their ties to the community are their primary sources of emotional support.

And even those women who do enter into their retirement in the bosom of a family aren't likely to leave it in quite the same way. The brutal truth is that the popular stereotype of the lonely widow reflects an important statistical reality. Women in North American society typically live several years longer than men. They typically marry men who are older than they are, and they can expect to live out the last years of their retirement without their spouse. Some women will form new partnerships. But we know that there are more women of retirement age than men, so finding a new age-peer mate of the opposite sex becomes more of a challenge the older we get. If we're smart, even if we're surrounded now by a loving family, we won't put all our eggs in one basket. We may dream of an endless retirement with the spouse we love, but we have to be prepared for the possibility that that won't happen. It's only realistic to put some priority on the cultivation of other relationships.

And even if in the midst of family life, we've always had others in our lives who are close to us. If we fail to nurture those relationships, if we fail to cultivate new ones like them, we'll be seriously shortchanging ourselves. We'll be turning our backs on a mother lode of emotional sustenance, intellectual stimulation, social support, love, trust — the list is endless! The gifts we get and give in forming and nurturing human relationships are essential to our identity as human beings.

So where do we start building our retirement community?

GRIEVING OUR LOSSES
Unmoored From the Workplace

For many of us, work supplied most of our non-family relationships, as well as generating our professional identity. We don't want to romanticize work relationships. They aren't always trouble free, and for some of us they were toxic, and tipped the balance towards early retirement — we had to get away! But more typically, the workplace provides a ready-made, low-maintenance network of people with lots in common. For many of us, our lives have been so crowded that it's the only social circle we've had time to cultivate. As we contemplate retirement, we realize that our relationships with our colleagues at work will be gone, or at least fundamentally altered. And that's scary. Once that workplace link is gone, what next? However much time and energy we have invested in our workplace relationships, we know that they are delicate hybrids and may not survive outside the work environment. The workplace was a community, where our days were filled with familiar tasks and duties. And now the essential glue that held us together with our workmates will be dissolved. Now we'll no longer be in the loop of day-to-day work. We'll no longer be part of the in-group around the water cooler. We may get together with our former colleagues regularly for lunch, but we won't have the daily coinage to spend with those still remaining at the job. We won't be there for the spontaneous get-togethers after work. Leaving work means leaving a whole social structure, which gave us importance and presence and connectedness, which gave shape and meaning to our lives.

The loss of our workplace community may be the first traumatic loss of retirement. We still want to feel connected and useful. We still want to engage in meaningful work. We do not want retirement to end the pleasures we share with others. We will have to find new communities to realize these needs.

Should we try to maintain workplace relationships? When you retire, promising to "stay in touch" is part of the ritual leave-taking. But is it a good idea? Is it better to make a clean break with our working lives, and move on, building a new social circle to go with our new retired selves?

The simple answer, of course, is that you should stay in touch with your old workplace friends *if you want to*. Not all workplace colleagues were friends, and not all workplace friendships are forever. But if you do want to keep those friendships, just remember that your workmates, unless you all retired together, are still caught in the maelstrom. They're busier than you are. That doesn't mean they won't be delighted to meet you for lunch or a drink after work or a weekend in the country. But it does mean you'll probably have to work a little harder at it — the initiative may have to come from you. Don't sulk and feel hurt if they don't call you, even when they promised they would. If they're still important to you, make the call yourself. And if they get too busy and have to cancel a lunch date, don't take it personally. You did it yourself and had it done to you often enough when you were working full time. You know what the working world is like. So by all means, keep up your old work relationships and friendships, if you want to.

That's the simple answer. But there's a more complex answer too. And to find it, you have to ask yourself what your motivation is for keeping in touch. Are you just hanging on to the shreds of an old identity and not getting on with the development of a new one? Remember, there's a whole world of other possibilities out there. For example, if you follow our advice, you'll be developing a work plan for your retirement. You'll be entering a whole new world of work — paid or unpaid. We already know that common work helps us identify common interests. It's the same in retirement. Whatever we "do," whether it's paid work, volunteering, education, travel, or hobbies, work will probably be our most fruitful source of new relationships. Pay attention to the people you meet now. Some of them will help you establish your new self, and become an important part of your new life.

Dislocated

At least as conventionally defined, retirement means leaving the workplace, and with it the workplace community. Retirement may also mean, or bring with it, a move out of our familiar neighborhood — a double loss. Leaving a community of familiar routines and activities can be very difficult. We know the place. We are part of the rhythm. We talk to neighbors and get the news as we exchange greetings. We get to know where things are and who occupies our space with us. We can access goods and services easily.

We do not want retirement to end these social contacts and the comforting sense of belonging and connectedness that comes with them. These can be wrenching emotional leavings. If they are voluntary and carefully planned, they may be less so, but if precipitated by circumstances beyond our control, they may be very discomforting. Finding new communities that satisfy these psychological and social needs will be an integral part of our new jobs as retired women.

CONSOLIDATING OUR GAINS
Women's Friendships

Luckily, we've got other friendships. Some of our friendship-building skills may be rusty. But we know how to do it. We've been doing it all our lives.

Who's your best friend? Does this sound like something from the schoolyard? It may actually date back to then. Some of us have female friends from public school that we have cherished right up to today. We have shared milestones, dates, and secrets with these women. We've laughed and cried with them. We know all about their family medical troubles, dining room paint color, and shoe size. We talk on the telephone regularly and might even have their salad bowl in our dish drainer from last night's shared dinner. These are longstanding and enduring relationships that have stood the test of time. We can rely on each other. We've been there for each other over the long haul.

Who else is around in your life? What about your roommate in university? You hit it off and spent time together, went to the same classes, socialized right through to graduate school. Now you live in different cities, but keep in touch by e-mail. You wouldn't think of not sending her a postcard from your next major holiday. You have memorized her postal code, you've used it so much. You still use the shawl she sent you for some birthday. Your conversations take on a serious note — you discuss ideas, not everyday details. You've shared all the stuff about breast cancer and menopause, and she is much more adventurous than you are with naturopathy. She stays with you when she can and you make little visits by yourself just to spend time with her when you need a break. She's your friend.

And your neighbors? You've lived side-by-side for many years. You know about the schedule at her parents' cottage. You know they're having some financial problems. You know one of them is thinking separation. They know you have rediscovered yoga. They've had your house keys for ages and they watch out for the mail and flyers on the front porch when you are out of town. You brought in their recycling bins when you passed their house this morning because you know they are away. You trust them and they trust you. You've learned to get along and you'd help each other in a jam. These are women you can think of as another concentric ring of friends as your circle goes wider.

Don't take this question of friendship lightly. Take inventory.

- Look in your personal address/phone book and see who you have on rapid dial
- List your women friends
- Rank them in "closeness"
- Describe the support you can count on them for — from experience
- Describe the support you give them
- Who would you call right now if you were in the emergency ward?
- Who has a spare set of keys to your house?

- Who do you tell first about your holiday? Who do you send postcards to?
- Where do your friends live?
- How often do you see each other?
- How old are your friends — older *and* younger?
- What do you need to change?

Cherish the friends in your life. You'll want them around in your retirement.

Relationships Aren't Always Friendships

Not all relationships are friendships, but they can be essential all the same. There is a whole cast of people that you look forward to seeing in specific contexts — the cottage, perhaps, or the local library. They may not meet all your criteria for intimate friendship, but you like them and they honor your presence in their lives by being available for enjoyable but limited encounters and activities. There is the one you can call when the book readers' conference is on in town. The one who can get you into a bridge game. The one who can format and knows everything about fonts. The people at church who are always so generous. What about the film buff who always tries to get you to go to foreign films? These people will be increasingly important to you as you are establishing your new identity as a retired woman. Honor them and they will honor you.

NEW LIFE, NEW RELATIONSHIPS
A Note of Caution

You will need new people around you to share this new part of your life. One wonderful thing about our changed lives and new activities is the possibility of making new friends. Old friendships are precious, but new ones may serve as ideal models and facilitators for our new retirement identity. We will encounter new dynamics for forming relationships and identity. We must, of course, be watchful for those who try to pull us into the same stagnant dynamics that might have mired us in family or older friendships — old habits die hard. Successful new relationships will be based on shared values, mutual interest, respect, reciprocity, and genuine affection. This is a time for establishing a new wholeness and integrity in our lives.

Now you have the time to cultivate your acquaintances, and explore whether you want to redefine them as friends. But don't forget that it can work in reverse as well. Maybe you need to do a little house-cleaning among your relationships. Feel free to ditch the woman who only mooches symphony tickets. Get rid of the one who never calls you when she has an extra ticket to the ballet. Dump the one who has never understood reciprocity. Insist that she return your favorite CD from her bottomless pit of discs she never listens to. Stop going to the hairdresser who is getting sloppy and not listening anymore, just because you have been going to her for ages. You have no time in your new retired identity for these draining relationships.

Male Friends and the Single Sixty

You have time now for male friends too. You've already had male friends — both inside and outside the workplace. Even if you're happily part-nered, there are likely men who have served as mentors and advisors in your life, and vice versa. You've taught them about shopping for deals, using their microwaves, and buying no-iron shirts. They may be welcome sources of information and doers of small tasks into your life. You've accompanied them to parties and weekday movie matinees. Sometimes you get matched up with them by hostesses who want even numbers at dinner parties. Sparks didn't fly, but you got to be friends instead.

Or maybe sparks did fly. Or you'd like them to now. It used to be a taboo subject, but there's lots written now about sex and the older woman. One of the best books on the issue is Gail Sheehy's *Sex and the Seasoned Woman*. She reminds us that we needn't hang up our hot pants, just because we're not twenty-one any more. She also reminds us that there's a sizzling singles scene to be found for the over-fifties and sixties throughout the land. If you're recently single, you may need to be reminded that you do not have to cohabit with a partner for sex and intimacy to be an important and meaningful part of your life. Do not give up on this if it is a vital part of your life. What you do is your business, your choice.

Many women will mourn lost spouses. Most of these will likely learn to accommodate themselves to a more solitary existence and a new identity as a single person. Others, newly widowed or divorced, will have a harder time coming to terms with the identity of being single. If they believe they need a permanent partner as a source of fulfillment, they will work toward that end. Some of them will be lucky and find what they need. Others, sadly, will simply have to accept the fact that the demographic statistics are not in their favor.

Sexy: The New Cultural Stereotype for Older Women

If a new sexual relationship is the last thing you're interested in right now, you may find the hype about the sexy sexagenarian to be just another irritating media myth sent to plague you. You've probably heard, now that the first wave of boomers is hitting sixty, that "sixty is the new forty" (or even, according to some optimists, the new thirty-five!). There has been a spate of new books and newspaper articles dedicated to the proposition that boomer women are *hot*. Very hot! And they're not talking about hot flashes (although menopause, in its own way, is also very hot these days). Isn't the latest term "cougars?" Older women on the prowl for younger men?

Many of us have very mixed feelings about all of this. The cultural stereotype of the older woman as hag, socially and sexually undesirable, clearly needed to be jettisoned. That prejudice robbed women of the confidence they had earned from their life experience, and stood between them and a whole host of potential romantic relationships as they got older — relationships between older men and older women, between older women and younger men, between older women and younger women. It also stood in the way of intergenerational friendships, since younger people were programmed to believe that older women were washed up, and had little to offer in a relationship.

But the new stereotype of the Sexy Sixties is the usual double-edged sword for women. It offers scope and credibility for the continuing vitality of older women in all areas of their lives, including sex and romance, but at the same time it also adds new pressure, with the subliminal message that if older women can be hot, they *should* be hot. If you're not, you're not trying hard enough.

Bombarded with the media propaganda, do you get an eerie sense of déjà vu? Remember when you were sixteen? Remember *Seventeen* and its sister magazines, relentlessly peddling an unattainable image of perfect young womanhood that we were programmed to covet, and did covet? We paid a heavy price for buying into the fantasy — years of tears and crash diets and low self-esteem, and product after product guaranteed to turn the frog into the fairy princess. Is it happening again?

With the help of the women's movement (and for some of us, years of therapy!) we escaped all that. Now we love ourselves just the way we are. Let's not fall into the same old trap all over again.

Internet Friendships

We have observed with delight the new phenomenon of blogs and interactive websites that connect older women. The forthrightness, practicality, and helpfulness of these networks are truly amazing. They appear to foster a special breed of friendship, reminiscent of dialogues with strangers on long train rides, where confidences are openly shared in a non-threatening environment. There are single-purpose chat rooms where women can trade practical advice on widowhood, home repairs, and health or beauty tips. Some diligence is required in surfing the net, and we advise the usual cautions in providing too much identifying information, for safety reasons. It is hard to single out websites because the universe of the blog is very fluid and the interests of women vary so dramatically. To get a feel for what's out there, you should check out a couple of key sites hosted by prominent older women: www. suzannebraunlevine.com (Suzanne Braun Levine's blog) and www. seasonedwomansnetwork.com (Gail Sheehy's blog). Your search engine will help you locate many, many more.

COMMUNITY IN OUR LIVING ARRANGEMENTS
Living Alone

> I live in that solitude which is painful in youth, but delicious in the years of maturity.
>
> Albert Einstein, *Out of My Later Years*, 1950

Almost 40 percent of women sixty-five and over live alone. This may or may not be a welcome development. After years of living with others constantly present, some women welcome the solitude. Alone at last, in one's own place! They enjoy the control they can have over what occupies their space, and the freedom to choose what to do, what to wear, what and when to eat, without consulting anyone but themselves.

Not all of us, however, are happy to live alone. Women are social beings who enjoy routines of daily contact with others. And if living alone is your choice, there are still some questions that must be answered. Are you confident that neighbors and friends will be reliable in times of need? Who will you depend on for help with simple errands, or maintenance and repairs? Can you afford to pay for help if friends and family aren't nearby to rally round?

Living alone does not mean being unproductive. An artist or dressmaker will be able, perhaps for first time, to spread out painting and sewing projects long set aside because of domestic arrangements. The freedom to read all night and sleep all day, if the novel is a can't-put-down thriller, can be a wonderful new luxury. And if your spouse never wanted a pet, now might be the time for you to acquire a cat, a bird, or a dog.

Living alone can mean social isolation, which is often thought of as the most worrisome part of retirement. Some retired women cite safety concerns as part of their need to be around others, not because of any physical threat of violence, but because they want to know they can reach out to someone "just in case," or when a little reassurance is needed. Women worry about falls in the bathroom, kitchen fires, and sudden illness. While some of these concerns can be allayed by visiting homecare workers, there is nothing like the sound of a human voice or the presence of a friend to relieve anxiety. Knowing that friendly chance encounters are likely to occur seems to be important for women. Also, the opportunity to share information and just "check in" with someone can be just enough to make living alone satisfying.

Women with health issues who live alone should consider subscribing to services such as Lifeline, which fit clients with an easy-to-use personal alarm device to wear as a necklace or bracelet. Just press the button any time of the night or day and an alarm linked to your name and address will sound in the monitoring office. If Lifeline is unable to contact you, they will contact listed family members or neighbors immediately.

Even the occasional woman who is happily partnered may have a hankering to live on her own. One example is Carolyn Heilbrun, a Columbia University professor and best-selling author of the Kate Fansler mystery series. At age sixty-eight, happily married, and living in New York City, she decided to buy a house of her own in the country. Eventually her husband came to share this space with her, but on her terms. She discusses this in her engaging and poignant short memoir, *The Last Gift of Time: Life Beyond Sixty,* The Dial Press, New York 1997.

Failing that, emergency services will be dispatched to your house. The cost of the Lifeline service is about $40 per month, after a one-time set-up fee. Check it out at www.lifeline.ca. Lifeline operates Canada-wide. Similar local services can also be found in most communities.

If you have just recently retired, or are just planning to retire, you may not have a very clear picture about what life is like in your neighborhood between nine and five on a weekday. Try this experiment. See what it is like to be home during the day. Will you be totally alone in a commuter community, the streets empty after the last office worker has left for the train? Are you okay with this, or does it make you feel abandoned? Lonely? Afraid? After you have read the paper and washed your coffee cup, what will you do? And who will you do it with? If solitude works for you in your current community, great! If it doesn't, try something else — one of the space-sharing alternatives we discuss below, or perhaps even a retirement community such as we discussed in Chapter 7.

Maybe you have always wanted to live somewhere else. Now that you are retired and on your own, you feel ready. Once again, you should experiment — look before you leap. Try taking an extended holiday in your chosen location, to see if life alone there is as good as it was when you were partnered, as good as you thought it might be. Just pulling up all your roots right now might not be the best thing you can do. Take your time.

How you feel about having others around you is something only you can know. How close you want others to be and who these others will be has to be your decision.

Sharing Spaces: Alternatives to Living Alone

> One of the oldest human needs is having someone to wonder where you are when you don't come home at night.
>
> Attributed to Margaret Mead

Having our own private quarters in a constellation with other independent individuals may be an attractive option for some of us. This can be in an ordinary apartment or townhouse in your chosen location. There's lots of variety in these housing complexes. Do you want to live mostly with older adults? Do you want to be with families? Do you want a pool and an exercise facility? Do you need a balcony or access to outdoors? You choose. But choose carefully.

One concept that seems to work well is forming a group that lives and works at their passion together. There are artist groups that have created cooperatives for living and working together. Some just rent space to work in; others prefer a live/work combination. They likely started with like-minded individuals getting together because they wanted to; you might find a space there.

Women friends have also joined together in cooperatives where each has her own private area, but shares communal spaces and meal times with others. These arrangements are becoming more common. These co-ops offer privacy and personal space as well as the options of shared space and activities. Close friends, who know each other well enough to plan for contingencies of personality, can often come to a mutually agreed living arrangement based on either social or financial imperatives.

Or you might want to consider a "feminary," a concept that is taking root in some urban centers. These are larger residential facilities established *by* women, *for* women. Feminaries, by definition, are based on feminist principles and have a collaborative, "sisterhood" approach to communal living. With attention paid to shared values, they are sensitive to the differing financial circumstances of their residents, and offer a broad range of supportive capabilities and services. Feminaries haven't yet been in existence long enough to have a track record, but they have the potential to be a very attractive living alternative.

The Toronto-based Older Women's Network (OWN) undertook a research study in 1998 on the housing needs of mid-life and older women in a number of southern Ontario communities. Not surprisingly, its findings were troublesome — the needs of these women are not being met in the housing marketplace. OWN responded to this research report with a number of useful recommendations to government, but also with a couple of co-operative housing projects of its own targeted at older women. For more information, consult the OWN website: www.older-womensnetwork.org.

Finding Community: Your New Social Circle

Each of us has already built a loosely defined community — a community made up of our friends and acquaintances, our colleagues, our families. Our membership in that community is essential to our identity. As we work through our plans for retirement, we're likely to find that we'll assemble our new retirement social circle the same way we built our previous one, the old-fashioned way — by solidifying older relationships that still meet our needs and satisfy our spirit, by being open to new experiences and new people, by understanding that meaningful and enduring relationships require tolerance and reciprocity. We'll make new friends — lots of them. Friends from our old lives. Friends from all the rich new facets of our new lives. Friends of all ages. "Be a good friend, get a good friend" is a mantra that will guide us well in our search for sustaining relationships in retirement.

But in addition to friendships, we may also find a place and an identity in our community as an "elder." Some of our new emerging identity as a retired person may be derived from our "emeritus" professional status, from continuing productive accomplishment, community activities, and volunteer work. We'll evolve, if we're open to playing this role, into the woman others turn to for advice, counsel, a shoulder to cry on, or a willing ear. We'll be the woman who knows about plant selection, a cheap and clean place to stay in New York, or what to do with a gift of fresh gooseberries. We'll be the font of all wisdom on what it's like to volunteer for different agencies, or which agencies treat their volunteers best. We may find enormous satisfaction in having these sorts of identities in the community.

Your own needs and interests will determine which networks of relationships will be in your life. The important thing is that there is no need to be lonely or to wait for friends to come to you. It's up to you to seek out your new community. Your relationship plan is an indispensable part of your retirement plan.

CHAPTER 16

Redefining Retirement: Are We There Yet?

OUR OWN RETIREMENT JOURNEY

When we began writing this book, both of us were contemplating retirement after successful professional careers. We had lots of questions, concerns, and issues about this looming life passage. So did our women friends and Margret's patients. And we couldn't find a lot of help out there. There were books about retirement, of course, lots of them. But most of them, still stuck in the old "male breadwinner" ways of thinking about work, retirement, and family life simply weren't for us. There were books about financial planning, and some of them were even specifically targeted to women. But those books didn't tell us much about retirement beyond how to pay for it — if we were lucky. They didn't give us the woman-centered, integrated approach to working out retirement issues that we needed to prepare us for the next stage of our lives. To the extent that they reflected the realities of the New Retirement at all, the mirror they held up was not one in which we, as women, could see ourselves reflected.

During the writing process, our own retirements have been a work in progress. We've been on different voyages of personal discovery.

Margret has cut back on her clinical psychology practice, but she hasn't let go altogether, and has no plans to do so. She now chairs the boards of several non-profit organizations and has become interested in issues of governance. Elizabeth has left the private practice of law — most likely for good — but has embarked on a full-time doctoral program back at law school. Her plans for the future do not include withdrawing from active engagement with life any time soon, although they do include a better work-life balance than she enjoyed in private practice.

So, Are We Retired?

Maybe. We're still working on our money plans, work plans, health and relationships plans. In the process, we've both learned a lot about ourselves and our relationship with our work. And we've learned that the New Retirement for women will be different things to different people. We've learned that retirement isn't a one-time event, a single step over a clear black line — it's a journey. That journey begins for every woman when she reaches a certain age and stage in life, and starts re-evaluating her relationship with work, with time, with her body, with her family and her community. Where will that journey take you? Only you can say. You've got to custom-design your own retirement. And because it's a custom design, it's also a custom definition.

Maybe you fit snugly into the Statistics Canada definition we talked about in Chapter 1. You're in your late fifties, you're not in the labor force, you receive more than half your income from retirement-like sources. And you think of yourself as retired. Or maybe that definition doesn't work for you at all. Maybe you're only fifty, you just left a twenty-five-year career as an accountant, you don't have a pension, and you've taken another job in a florist shop, but you *do* think of yourself as retired. Or maybe you fit the profile, but you *don't* think of yourself as retired; you see yourself as simply between jobs. Are you retired or aren't you? Nobody can answer that question but you. It's your own definition of retirement that you must honor.

A QUESTION OF IDENTITY

In Chapter 2, we talked about our fear that we'll suffer an identity crisis when we're out of the work force and on our own. We talked about the extent to which our jobs have come to define who we are and how society measures our value by what we do for money. And we talked about how we come to value *ourselves* by the same yardstick. We gave voice to the concern we all share, that when we cease to be working people, we may become invisible. We may cease to be *us*.

Through our work, we forged certain identities: as teacher, as nurse, as lawyer, as psychologist. These identities have only been part of who we are, of course; we have also played roles in our families, and in our communities. As Freud so famously said, "Love and work are the cornerstones of our humanness." We have played many roles throughout our lives, and when one role comes to an end, we find a new one. In retirement, we are free to make new identities and to redefine ourselves. We may encounter some resistance from family members and friends and colleagues as we struggle to change roles that may have worked better for them than they did for us. But this is "our time," and we alone must define who we will be in retirement.

We have taken you through a process of defining and designing a retirement that can vanquish your fears of loss of identity, a retirement that will help you to find and foster your own unique self as a woman retired from the work force. How will you know when you have succeeded?

Imagine this scenario. The time is in your future, but perhaps that future is not very distant. You are at a social event, enjoying yourself. This is your coming-out as a retired person. A complete stranger asks you, in a friendly way, "What do you do?" How will you answer?

Let's rehearse the conversation. But first, let us set your inner scenario. This is where you want to be in retirement. Happy, confident, enjoying yourself. Clear in your purpose. This is where all your plans converge.

Fill in your own blanks — our prompts will give you the idea, but you're working off your own retirement plan here.

You've thought about it, planned it, worked towards it, and now you are living it. You're ready to reply to the stranger. Start your answer: "I am retired and I…"

"I'm retired."

"I used to … (work as a lawyer, work as a psychologist, drive a bus, be married, live in Sudbury)."

"I left all that behind because I … (found it too stressful, never had time to do what I really wanted, was becoming bored and stale, wanted to try something different, realized it was my life and it was now or never, just thought it was time)."

"Now I'm … (planning a trip to Nepal, learning Chinese, reading all the Canadian novels I can get my hands on, buying a lathe, taking up Pilates, rediscovering my husband, starting my own business as a caterer)."

"I've had lots of help from … (my family, my friends, the members of my volleyball team, this great book I just read on retirement!)."

"I can't believe … (that I waited so long, that I thought I couldn't do it on so little money, that I'd ever like golf, that it would be so much fun, that I'd meet so many interesting women in the same boat, that I'm a grandmother)."

"I feel … (so happy, so free, so busy!)"

You're self-assured and confident, you've had lots of interesting things to say, and you leave that conversation feeling good about yourself. You've made it. You know who you are again. You've carved out your place in the universe for the next phase of your life. You can look forward to the future.

You're retired!

Everything flows, and nothing is left unchanged.

Greek philosopher Heraclitus, *Panta Rei*

FURTHER Reading

CHAPTER 1

Brown, Rosemary. *The Good NonRetirement Guide 2006*. London, UK: Kogan Page, 2006.

Costa, Dora L. *The Evolution of Retirement: An American Economic History 1880-1990*. Chicago, IL: University of Chicago Press, 2000.

Kotlikoff, Laurence K., and Scott Burns. *The Coming Generational Storm: What You Need to Know About America's Economic Future*. Cambridge, MA: MIT Press, 2005.

O'Donnell, Jill, Graham McWaters and John A. Page. *The Canadian Retirement Guide: A Comprehensive Handbook on Aging, Retirement, Caregiving and Health*. Toronto, ON: Insomniac Press, 2006.

Savishinsky, Joel S. *Breaking the Watch: The Meanings of Retirement in America*, Ithaca, NY: Cornell University Press, 2002.

Warner, Ralph. *Get a Life: You Don't Need a Million to Retire Well*, 5th edition. Berkeley, CA: Nolo, 2004.

Zelinski, Ernie. *How to Retire Happy, Wild, and Free: Retirement Wisdom You Won't Get from Your Financial Advisor*, Edmonton, AB: Visions International Publishing, 2004.

CHAPTER 2
Dychtwald, Ken, and Daniel J. Kadlec. *The Power Years: A User's Guide to the Rest of Your Life*. Mississauga, ON: John Wiley & Sons, 2006.

Levine, Suzanne Braun. *Inventing the Rest of Our Lives: Women in Second Adulthood*. New York, NY: Viking 2005.

Neugarten, Bernice. *The Meaning of Age: Selected Papers*. Chicago, IL: University of Chicago Press, 1996.

CHAPTER 3
Dominguez, Joe and Vicki Robin. *Your Money or Your Life: Transforming Your Relationship with Money and Achieving Financial Independence*. New York, NY: Penguin Books, 1992.

Eisenberg, Lee. *The Number: A Completely Different Way to Think About the Rest of Your Life*. New York, NY: Simon & Schuster/Free Press, 2006.

Longacre, Doris Janzen. *Living More With Less: A Pattern for Living With Less and a Wealth of Practical Suggestions From the Worldwide Experience of Mennonites*. Waterloo, ON: Herald Press, 1980.

Pape, Gordon. *The Retirement Time Bomb* Toronto, ON: Penguin Group (Canada), 2005.

CHAPTER 4

Townson, Monica. *Independent Means: A Canadian Woman's Guide to Pensions and a Secure Financial Future.* Toronto, ON: MacMillan Canada, 1997.

Roseman, Ellen. *Money 101: Every Canadian's Guide to Personal Finance; Money 201: More Personal Finance Advice for Every Canadian* (Toronto ON: John Wiley & Sons, 2003).

CHAPTER 6

Mostowyk, Cathie, et al. *Shoestring Shopping Guide.* Toronto, ON: Cybercom Publishing. Updated annually.

Long, Charles. *How to Survive Without a Salary: Learning How to Live the Conservor Lifestyle.* Toronto, ON: Warwick Publishing, 2006.

Levine, Judith. *Not Buying It: My Year Without Shopping.* New York, NY: Simon & Schuster/Free Press, 2006.

CHAPTER 7

Cleveland, Joan. *Everything You Need to Know About Retirement Housing.* New York, NY: Penguin Books, 1996.

CHAPTER 8

Moses, Barbara. *What Next? The Complete Guide to Taking Control of Your Working Life.* London, UK: Dorling Kindersley Publishing, 2003.

Rifkin, Jeremy. *The End of Work.* New York, NY: Tarcher Putnam, 1995.

Pollan, Stephen M., and Mark Levine. *Second Acts: Creating the Life you Really Want, Building the Career You Truly Desire.* New York, NY: Harper Collins, 2003.

Bolles, Richard. *What Color Is Your Parachute? 2007: A Practical Manual for Job Hunters and Career Changers.* Berkeley, CA: Ten Speed Press, 2006.

CHAPTER 9

Cumyn, Alan. *What in the World Is Going On.* Ottawa, ON: Canadian Bureau of International Education, 2001. Download from www.destineduction.ca.

Hachey, Jean-Marc. *The BIG Guide to Living and Working Overseas,* 4th Edition. Toronto, ON: Intercultural Systems/Systemes Interculturel (ISSI), 2005, with free internet updates to 2008. (Formerly titled *The Canadian Guide to Living and Working Overseas.* Available in print from the University of Toronto Press, or online by subscription. Much of it can also be accessed free at www.workingoverseas.com.)

Human Resources Development Canada. *10 Essentials to Get That Job: An Employment Guide for the Experienced Worker,* Human Resources Development Canada, 2001.

Mediacorp Canada Inc. *Who's Hiring ...* Toronto, ON: Mediacorp Canada Inc. Appears annually.

Mediacorp Canada Inc. *Canadian Directory of Search Firms.* Toronto, ON: Mediacorp Canada Inc. Appears annually.

Walker, Jean Erickson. *The Age Advantage: Making the Most of Your Midlife Career Transition*. New York, NY: Berkley, 2000.

Watters, Marge, and Lynne O'Connor. *It's Your Move: A Personal and Practical Guide to Career Transition and Job Search for Canadian Managers, Professionals and Executives*. Toronto, ON: Harper Collins, 2004.

Foreign Affairs Canada, Consular Services. *Working Abroad, Unravelling the Maze*. Ottawa, ON: Foreign Affairs Canada, 2005. Also available at www.voyage.gc.ca.

Foreign Affairs Canada, Consular Services. *Her Own Way: Advice for the Woman Traveller*. Ottawa, ON. Also available at www.voyage.gc.ca.

CHAPTER 10
Campbell, Don. *Real Estate Investing in Canada*. Toronto, ON: John Wiley & Sons, 2005.

Edwards, Paul and Sarah Edward. *The Best Home Businesses for People 50+*. New York, NY: Tarcher/Penguin, 2004.

Good, Walter S. *Building a Dream: A Canadian Guide to Starting Your Own Business*. Toronto, ON: McGraw-Hill Ryerson, 2003.

Gray, Douglas, and Diana Gray. *The Complete Canadian Small Business Guide*, 3rd edition. Toronto, ON: McGraw-Hill Ryerson, 2000.

Kerr, Margaret, and JoAnn Kurtz. *Canadian Small Business Kit For Dummies*. Toronto, ON: For Dummies, 2007.

Stephenson, James. *202 Ways to Supplement Your Retirement Income.* Newburgh, NY: Entrepreneur Press, 2005.

CHAPTER 11

Kelley, Rob. *The Complete Guide to a Creative Retiremen*t. Austin, TX: Turnkey Press, 2003.

Cronin, Lynda. *Midlife Runaway: A Grown-Ups' Guide to Taking a Year Off.* Toronto, ON: MacMillan of Canada, 2000.

Rogers, Susan Fox, ed. *Solo: On her Own Adventure.* Toronto, ON: Seal Books, 2005.

Ausenda, Fabio, ed. *Green Volunteers: The World Guide to Voluntary Work on Nature Conservation.* New York, NY: Universe, 2005.

Schultz, Patricia. *1000 Places to See Before You Die: A Traveler's Life List.* New York, NY: Workman Publishing, 2003.

CHAPTER 12

Nelson, Miriam. *Strong Women Stay Young.* New York, NY: Bantam Books, 2005.

———. *Strong Women, Strong Hearts.* New York, NY: Perigee/Penguin, 2006.

———. *Strong Women and Men Beat Arthritis.* New York, NY: Berkeley Books/Penguin, 2003.

———. *Strong Women, Strong Bones: Everything You Need to Know to Prevent, Treat and Beat Osteoporosis,* New York, NY: Perigee/Penguin, 2006.

Weed, Susan. *The New Menopausal Years, The Wise Woman's Way.* Woodstock, NY: Ash Tree Publishing, 1992.

Cobb, Janine O'Leary. *Understanding Menopause.* Toronto, ON: Key Porter Books, 2005.

Philips, Dr. Robin, ed. *The Menopause Bible: The Complete Practical Guide to Managing Your Menopause.* Richmond Hill, ON: Firefly Books, 2005.

Olshansky, S. Jay, and Bruce A. Carnes. *The Quest for Immortality: Science at the Frontiers of Aging.* New York, NY: W.W. Norton & Co., 2001.

Rowe, John W., and Robert L. Kahn. *Successful Aging.* New York, NY: Dell, 1999.

Canadian Institute for Health Information. *Women's Health Surveillance Report: A Multi-Dimensional Look at the Health of Women in Canada.* CPHI, 2003. Available at www.cihi.ca or www.hc-sc.gc.ca.

Sheehy, Gail. *Menopause, The Silent Passage.* New York, NY: Simon & Schuster, 1998.

CHAPTER 13
Wister, Andrew V. *Baby Boomer Health Dynamics: How Are We Aging?* Toronto, ON: University of Toronto Press, 2005.

Peeke, Pamela. *Fight Fat After Forty.* New York, NY: Penguin, 2001.

Ezrin, Sharyn Salsberg. *Living Through Transitions.* Victoria, BC: Trafford Publishing, 2005.

CHAPTER 14

Rando, Therese A. *Grieving: How to Go on Living When Someone You Love Dies.* New York, NY: Bantam Books, 1991.

Levinson, Deborah. *Surviving the Death of Your Spouse.* Oakland, CA: New Harbinger Press, 2004.

Curry, Cathleen L. *When Your Spouse Dies: A Concise and Practical Source of Help and Advice.* Notre Dame, IN: Ave Maria Press, 1990.

Cardy, Sandy. *The Cottage, the Spider Brooch, and the Second Wife.* Toronto, ON: ECW Press, 2003.

Schlossberg, Nancy K. *Retire Smart, Retire Happy.* Washington, DC: American Psychological Association, 2004.

Jacobs, Ruth Harriet. *Be an Outrageous Woman.* Toronto, ON: Harper Collins Canada, 1997.

CHAPTER 15

Yager, Jan. *Friendshifts: The Power of Friendship and How It Shapes Our Lives.* Stamford, CT: Hannacroix Creek Books, 1999.

Goodman, Ellen, and Patricia O'Brien. *I Know Just What You Mean: The Power of Friendship in Women's Lives.* New York, NY: Simon & Schuster, 2002.

Dailey, Nancy. *When Baby Boom Women Retire.* New York, NY: Praeger Paperbacks, 2000.

Bridges, William. *Transitions: Making Sense of Life's Changes*. Cambridge, MA: Da Capo Press, 2004.

Bauer-Maglin, Nan, and Alice Radosh eds. *Women Confronting Retirement, A Nontraditional Guide*. Pisataway, NJ: Rutgers University Press, 2003.

Levine, Suzanne Braun. *The Women's Guide to Second Adulthood*. New York, NY: Bloomsbury Publishing, 2005.

Sheehy, Gail. *Sex and the Seasoned Woman*. New York, NY: Random House, 2006.

Acknowlegments

I am greatly indebted to my patients, friends, and family. My patients are a continuing source of inspiration and courage. I am humbled by the privilege of their allowing me to be part of their life journeys. Thank you for igniting the spark of this book from our work together. My friends are a continuing blessing in my life. I try to be that in their lives. Thank you for believing in me. My family continually showers me with expressions of love. I am honored to be part of this family and try, in my fumbling ways, to return your affection. My husband Peter Warrian's boundless optimism and never-ending confidence in me, constantly surprises me and always makes me want to be the best I can be. Thank you, love you.

My mentors, teachers, and colleagues continue to help me in wonderful and creative ways to inform my practice of cognitive behavioral psychology. I hope I have done justice to your confidence in me as a psychologist and to this orientation. Any mistakes are from my own interpretations.

The women at Second Story Press made this book a reality. Thank you all for your expert guidance and support.

Margret Hovanec

In writing this book, I incurred many debts. I owe much to the working women I encountered throughout my career as a labor lawyer — teachers, nurses, engineers, optometrists, postal workers, clerical, service and factory workers, and many others — who showed me the world of work in all its complexities. Likewise I'm grateful to the women of my former law firm — lawyers, administrators and support staff, all of you. My life is richer for your friendship and collegiality.

My family has given unflagging support for this project. My sisters and sisters-in-law have been an important reference group — Kathy, the two Carolyns, Mariette, Michelle, Barbara, Kim, Lori, Rachel, and Jill, thank you all. My children Graeme and Christina have been enthusiastic and helpful throughout. My mother, Jean Shilton, has been generous with her considerable editing skills. She has always been my best role model, maintaining active engagement with life and the world while aging with grace. Thanks, Mum! And finally my incomparable husband, David Mackenzie, fed me much useful resource material from his own omnivorous reading, reviewed and commented on the manuscript, and provided encouragement, black coffee and a fine wine when needed. I truly wouldn't and couldn't have done it without you, David.

And a special thanks to Bob Baldwin, who lent his expertise in the midst of a very busy schedule to improve Chapter 4 (remaining errors, of course, are ours alone).

Elizabeth Shilton

About the Authors

Dr. Margret Hovanec is a psychologist and a Founding Fellow in the Academy of Cognitive Therapy. Margret is also Co-founder and Chair of the Board of The Lupina Foundation, a private foundation supporting research and innovation in the areas of health and society. She has taught cognitive therapy at the graduate level and has delivered presentations across North America and the United Kingdom. Margret is married and lives in Toronto, where she has a private practice. Her retirement is a work in progress.

Elizabeth Shilton is a lawyer. She was a founding and managing partner of one of Canada's leading labor and employment law firms, where she practiced law for twenty-five years, focusing on women's equality rights, education law, and pension and benefits law. She is currently working on pension policy research, and is a member of the Ontario Financial Services Tribunal. Elizabeth and her family divide their time between Toronto, Ontario and Gabian, France.